Surviving Bina's Secrets

A True Story of Abuse and Recovery in Africa and America

by Bina

Printed in the United States of America
ISBN: 978-1-937317-49-2

CATALOGING INFORMATION:

Bina

Surviving Bina's Secrets

A True Story of Abuse and Recovery in Africa and America

Filing categories:

BIO002010 BIOGRAPHY &
AUTOBIOGRAPHY/Cultural, Ethnic &
Regional/African American & Black

BIO022000 BIOGRAPHY &
AUTOBIOGRAPHY/Women

Table of Contents

Continued

The olive branch is a symbol of peace, harmony and hope. In biblical accounts, extending an olive branch meant the ending of hostilities between two parties and signaled the end of a conflict. I found it symbolic in telling my story, and my hope is that girls throughout the world will speak up and know that they deserve respect and happiness.

Preface

This is the story of my life I have written down on these pages—the bad and the good, but as you will read, mostly the bad. I don't remember some of it, but the people I've talked to have recounted my past. I used to be so embarrassed about it all, but I'm grown up now. I'm an old lady. It makes me kind of sick, but there's not too much I can do about it. I've been learning how to talk about it to make myself feel better.

I know that putting all of this down on paper has helped me a lot. It has helped take away the anger. I am very lucky that I have some good friends to talk to. Some of them are here in the U.S. and some are still on the islands. I kept this secret all of my life until after I turned 50. I do know I want to help children so they will not go through what I went through. I want all the young people to know that you should not wait until you are old to talk about what happens in your life. Find somebody to talk to. Don't keep it inside; don't keep it a secret. Find some way to deal with it or it will deal with you.

I wrote this book about my life to discover who I am. I want to let other women know what went on in my life every day. No one should have to live with the things that I put up with. Women need to speak up for themselves. I'm not embarrassed anymore. As a kid, I used to be afraid to go to school. I was afraid that people knew who my mother was and they would talk about me. When I was in school, I had a short attention span. I couldn't speak or hear very well. I hardly learned to read. My mom would beat me because I didn't want to go to school. I used to get sick every day. I have attended school here in the United States, but I usually do not stay long because I am suspicious that people are talking about me or making fun of me. My English is bad and my reading isn't very good either. But I think that the process of putting all the bad things that happened to me in this book has helped me like therapy. I can't afford any professional therapy, so, I guess this is the next best thing.

Chapter 1

EARLY YEARS

The Cape Verde Islands are located approximately 350 miles west off the coast of Africa and were owned by the government of Portugal. These islands were used as warehouses for slaves from other parts of Africa starting in the 1500s. The slaves were brainwashed by the natives of Portugal and were told that they were Portuguese, when in fact they were not—they were African. The Portuguese took over the area and brought their language and customs to the islands. It didn't matter if they were originally from Africa, or how kinky their hair was, they were told that they were Portuguese and made to believe it. There were many Africans who were already of mixed Portuguese and African descent. A lot of people started to learn that they were not really Portuguese, because they were being used as slaves.

My grandfather, Nako, came to the United States from Cape Verde when he was 18 years old to work for a better life. He was an African man who met and fell in love with the most beautiful woman—my grandmother. She was a mixture of French, Italian, and Creole living in the town of Plenty, Massachusetts. They got married and had two daughters—Linda (my mother) and her younger sister, Marvina. After having worked in the U.S. a few years, Grandfather felt that he could take his money, his family, and his belongings back to his homeland. Grandfather took Grandmother, who was pregnant with my Uncle José, and his two daughters back to Cape Verde where they could live more comfortably. After reaching the islands, my uncle was born and Grandmother died about four years later of natural causes. My grandfather found another woman to take the place of my grandmother and had several children with this woman.

Grandfather became a wealthy man and owned a lot of land on the island. He enjoyed fishing with Dominico, a man he thought was his best friend. One evening, the two of them went to their favorite fishing spot on the ocean rocks to fish by moonlight. They were not getting along very well, and began to argue about something. As my grandfather got near the edge of one of the rocks, Dominico pushed him and Grandfather fell into the water. When Dominico looked down into the deep ocean water for my

grandfather, he saw the water was full of blood. It was nearly three in the morning and Dominico left for home.

The next day someone asked him if he had seen his friend, Nako. Dominico said that Nako was dead. Later, neighbors told my mom's family that my grandfather had died at the fishing spot where he and Dominico had argued. Everyone knew that there would be no chance of Grandfather surviving a fall into the water, especially with the heavy overcoat he always wore while fishing. Several of my grandfather's friends went to the fishing spot to look for the body, but it was never found.

There was very little justice or law enforcement on the island to protect the innocent or apprehend the guilty. Dominico went unpunished and my mom lost her father at the age of eighteen. For me, it is sad that I never got to meet either of my grandparents. I could have learned so much about life from them.

GRANDFATHER AND MOTHER

My mother was three years old when she arrived to the islands; at least that's what other people told her. When her mother died, she was seven years old. She was eighteen when her father died. She was raised pretty much without a mother. I don't blame her completely for the things that happened to me growing up; I felt bad for her because of the situation she grew up with. Who knows what happened to her while she was growing up?

When my grandfather died, she lost everything and had to take care of herself. She was to go through many more trials and tribulations. My mom got pregnant and ended up losing four kids—three died and one was lost on the way to São Tomé. This daughter is the sister I am looking for. We don't know if she is alive or not.

My mother worked hard to make a living. She found out she had authorization to come to the U.S., but she didn't have the money to get there or to handle the paperwork. She had to have the right documents to prove who she was. It was especially hard for her without an education. The white people wanted to know all the information. I have nothing against white people; I know that they had more schooling and education than us blacks. I believe that

4

they were taking a lot of money from the poor people just for handling the paperwork to come to the U.S.

Because my mother didn't have the money, she had to find somebody who wanted to marry her so that she could legally live in the U.S. Then this man would pay all the expenses for them to go to the States. It took a long time. My mom held a lot of secrets; she kept them quiet so no one could talk about it. When Mom and I sat down to talk when I was older, we never seemed to talk without entering into our past, but we have a hard time talking about it. She had so much guilt in her that it showed when she was around my kids. She did so much for my kids that she never did when I needed her. She was there, but she was not there for me.

Sometimes I think my mom was abused when she was young. I feel I am like my mother in many ways. The way she sometimes reacted to trying to be a lady was a little strange. It makes me remember why I acted like that myself—it was my poor and abusive childhood. I cannot talk to her because my mom is over eighty years old and she doesn't like to talk about things like that. It is sad though, because I've heard some people say that if you have been abused, there is a chance that you will abuse also. But for me, I don't believe in that. I know for certain that I was abused, but what I have tried to do and I am doing is helping others to keep from being abused.

I never had any intention to abuse any child who came to my house. I couldn't. My heart just could not do it. My heart is ready to help. I know I'm a very lucky woman for what happened to me in my life. I'm still here and willing and able to help others. Any day, any time, anything that is needed from me, if I have it, I help people. This is one thing that can do people some good, especially children. Then again, I have always believed that if I had my grandparents, they would have taken me in. But that didn't happen. I don't even know what they looked like. It is sad sometimes.

Chapter 2
Maria Julia, 1942

In the 1940s there were severe droughts that caused famine throughout the islands. There were black bugs that ate up any crops that were grown. Only those who were really well off had enough saved up to be able to withstand those tough times. The poor people had to go where they could find work to feed their families. My mother's sister, Marvina, died with her family from the disease and hunger that ravaged the islands. My mother wanted to survive; she heard from other people about the opportunities to work in São Tomé, another island off of West Africa. She got a three-year work contract in 1942 to go there. Lina, a cousin of my younger sister, told me that her mom, Nana, didn't want my mother to take my sister, Maria Julia, away with her.

Auntie Nana told my mom, "Leave Maria Julia with me; I will take care of her. I will give her everything I

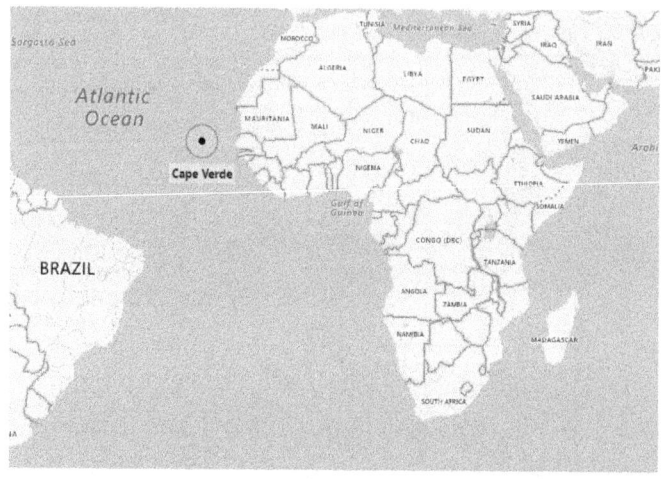

can and raise her the same way I raise my kids. I can take care of my kids and take care of her too!"

My mother said, "No way! I'm gonna take my daughter with me." But when my mother and her boyfriend took their daughter to the port, they discovered that there was only room for one more passenger. Since Mom had the contract to fulfill, she had to go and leave behind her beautiful little Maria Julia with the child's father, Marcos Luna. Maria Julia was of white complexion with blonde hair and beautiful blue eyes. She always wore a gold chain on her neck given to her by Marcos, because she was his only child and he gave her everything he could. She also wore gold earrings and was always dressed up because her father loved her very much.

Marcos was to look after Maria Julia and they were to leave several weeks later on the next ship to São

Tomé. There were no planes on the Cape Verde Islands, so they traveled by ship. It took approximately 30 days travel along the coast of Africa to reach São Tomé. Marcos got sick on this voyage and his illness lasted a long time. There was no medication and he had very little to eat. He eventually died before meeting up with my mother. They had no way to bury him, so they tossed his body into the Atlantic Ocean. My sister was only seven years old when she watched as they threw her father's body overboard. How frightened she must have felt, alone with no family to look after her—only these Creole people who were also on their way to find work in São Tomé.

We have reason to believe another family took her in and Maria Julia left with them from the boat as soon as it docked. My mother used to tell me about some of the people in that area who could not have children of their own. Some had a better life, but had no children. So, they would always go to the port to look for children when the ships arrived from other places with hungry people looking for work. Some of these families arrived so poor they would give away their children to a couple who could give their kids a better life. Some would even sell their children just to make some money.

Meanwhile, my mother waited for them to arrive with anticipation. Each day she went to work and at the end of the day she went by the port to look for them. She had to hurry back to her shed because she had a curfew after work. She wasn't sure when exactly they had departed from Cape Verde because she had no contact with her family. A ship's departure depended heavily on the weather and other circumstances.

Three months passed when one day she went to work and overheard a new co-worker talking to another co-worker. They talked about a man who died on the ship on his way to São Tomé. They said he left behind a seven-year-old daughter. This was when my mother discovered that it might have been Maria Julia and Marcos. My mom was heartbroken. She did not know what had become of Maria Julia. I can imagine my mother suffered terribly, not knowing where her little girl had gone. She tried desperately to find out what had happened to her. For three years she searched exhaustively, only to give up hope of ever seeing Maria Julia again. Many years later my mother told me that the day she heard the news about Maria Julia and Marcos was one of the most tragic days of her life.

Chapter 3
MOM AND DAD, 1943

Mother was saddened by the loss of her daughter and of her boyfriend's death. She still had to face the cruel task masters that would beat her whenever they thought she had not done the work correctly. I can imagine how angry she was that her life was so hard. Then in 1943, she met Roberto, the man who was to become my father. They lived together in the same house and had a little girl named Maria Rosa. Both of them wanted to leave São Tomé and return to their countries. My mother later told me that my father was from Angola, a large country in Africa. Lina told me that Mother used to always talk about my father. My father didn't want my mother to go back to the islands. Lina also said my mother talked about how good a person my father was; that he treated her so well. I don't understand why my mom would leave him to go back to the islands.

In 1946, Mother had to return to Cape Verde because her work contract had expired. When she returned to the islands of Cape Verde with Maria Rosa, she was about eight months pregnant with me. Roberto still had another six months to fulfill on his work contract before he could leave. A month or so later, I was born on the island of Fogo without my father there to help my mother.

When Roberto learned that he had to return to Angola, he wrote my mother a letter. Mother received the letter and responded with a letter of her own. She paid someone to deliver the letter to the post office. Later she found out that the courier did not deliver the letter; instead he destroyed it and kept the money. My mother and father lost contact, never to see each other again. I have never seen my father or any part of my father's family. Between my mother from the U.S. and my father from Angola, I am the only one born in the Cape Verde islands.

Three different names were given to me as my father's name. It wasn't my fault that I didn't know who my father was. It was just that there was no truthful communication between Mom and me. I believe she had a really hard life. She was pregnant and had nobody to help her; she had nobody at all. For a long time in the islands, if any girl became pregnant who wasn't married, the parents or the family completely ignored her. This was what happened when my uncles saw my mom pregnant with me. They didn't help her because she should've gotten married before she became pregnant.

Not too long ago, I wrote a letter to São Tomé where my father had worked and my older sister, Maria Julia, went missing. I wrote the letter to the attention of a lady named Armanda. I spoke to her by phone and she said she would do the best she could to help me find my father. It will be a big day in my life if ever I get to meet or see my father or my sister.

Chapter 4

Maria Bina is Born, 1946

The islands were beautiful, but sometimes it got very cold. Mom gave birth to me on November 1, 1946, in the village of Chardamarise in a little one-room house. The house was in the dirt and it was cold. Can you imagine how cold it was for a little baby? It was a little house, maybe 10 by 12 feet, covered only by tree branches and leaves. It was located on a big lot of land where the owners grew corn, potatoes, sweet potatoes, all kinds of beans, and vegetables. They also raised chickens, pigs, and cows.

That day when Mom began to give birth to me there was no family around to help. It happened that a man named Joãozinho passed by and heard Mom's groans and looked inside just in time to witness my birth. He picked me up off the floor and helped Mom get back to her bed. He put me in her arms and left, and was not to enter my life again until later under devastating circumstances. Mom had no money and had to find work. She had no one to take care of Maria Rosa and me. After a couple of days, she moved to a house in the village of Figerinha. This house was bigger, but we shared it with another family. The house would later become the school in this village, where I attended briefly. Mom had some relatives nearby who could take care of Maria Rosa while she went to work.

It's almost impossible to understand how poor things really were back in those times. I found out that Mom would leave me, a baby only a few days old, with the door unlocked. She left me alone from six in the morning till six in the evening, where anyone could walk in and take me. Maybe that was what she hoped for. Lina said that her mom used to give her food to feed me, like sweet potatoes, oatmeal, and rice. This was what they had for a week-old baby.

The lady next door had some young children, maybe first to third graders. Sometimes the parents would hear my crying and they would send one of these kids to feed me sweet potatoes and milk. Can you imagine a seven-year-old having to feed a one-week-old baby? And I don't know who would clean me, if they ever did. Maybe I cried because I was hungry and maybe sometimes I cried because I was dirty. It was bad enough to stay hungry all day until Mother got home in the evening. I was too young to remember all these things, but this is what I was told by some of the ladies who were there at that time.

They told me that they were the ones who fed me. I guess I call myself a survivor; I just refused to die. Maybe God had a plan for me to stay alive for some reason.

I was informed that my godfather, Jimmy, was very upset with my mom for leaving me alone while she went to work. She had to find a way to make a living. She went from house to house in the village and sometimes to other villages to work for food. Sometimes she would walk three to four hours just to sell wood in other towns. With the money she made, she bought clothes and necessities. It happened that my godfather passed by the house where we were staying and heard me crying. My godfather opened the door and found me all alone, crying without end. He picked me up and took me to Nana's house.

He notified her, "I'm gonna take this lady to the courts because she cannot leave this baby alone like this!"

Lina's mom explained to him, "You cannot do that to her. She's hungry, and she has to work for food to feed herself and her kids."

He responded, "This baby does not deserve to stay alone like this!"

So Nana said to my mom, "Bring this baby girl here. I'll feed her, clothe her, and I'll take care of her until you come home from work." However, my mom didn't want to do that because she thought it was too much for Nana, since she was already taking care of

Maria Rosa. I don't understand how my mom could take my three-year-old sister to Nana to care for, but could leave me all alone in the house while she went to work. Maybe Mom was afraid that Maria Rosa might harm me in some way, and that was why she did not take me along to Nana's house. Or, could it be that Mom didn't care about me like she did Maria Rosa? I think this because as I grew up, Mom never really showed any love for me.

It was in the early part of the summer of the following year when Auntie Nana asked my mom to come work for her during the corn harvest. Lina told me that when my mom took me to their house, she laid me down on top of a corn husk pile and I was almost lost. Lina's two brothers would make fun of me. They would tease my mom by warning, "Be careful with this kid of yours, because if the cat sees her, it's gonna swallow her like a mouse!"

Lina said I was so tiny and skinny; she thought I only weighed maybe a pound and a half. Lina also said that when I was six to seven months old, I was still very skinny, but I was strong. When they held my hands and tried to stand me up, I would try to walk. She said I would smile all the time and I liked to laugh. Even today I laugh a lot.

Lina said my mom use to go there to work for her mom. They had a better life because her mom's husband was in the U.S. and he would send them a lot of money. She recalled how her brothers would make fun of me.

They would say, "Take that thing out of here; I don't want to see her while I eat. It makes my stomach sick to see that thing!" I wonder if it was because I was ugly, or that I was skinny that I looked so bad to these older boys. They were almost young men—so full of life compared to me, such a little helpless thing.

When I was growing up, I heard things from other people that really hurt me. I remember people told me about Maria Rosa, my full-blood sister. Maria Rosa was just a little girl when Mother moved from São Tomé to the island of Fogo. It happened one day when Mom went to work for the widow Bebé in the nearby village of Boca de Founté. It was customary to harvest the corn, take off the husks, remove the corn from the cob and lay it out over the testerna, what we call a water-well. The cemented ceiling of the testerna, which covered the hidden water tank in the ground, was the best place to dry the corn.

Someone sent little Maria Rosa out to check on the chickens to make sure that they were not helping themselves to the corn. Maria Rosa went out and checked, and then she started to play like all young children do. She got up on top of the testerna cover over the well opening. The cover was made of wood and was very old and weathered. It was not strong enough to hold the weight of her little body. She was about three to four years old at the time when she broke through the cover and fell in.

As time passed, Mom started to miss her, so she went out to look for her. She called, "Maria, Maria!" and there was no answer. Others joined in the search for little Maria Rosa, but it took a while for them to finally discover she had fallen into the water well. Mom started screaming to get someone to go down into the testerna to get her baby girl. There were plenty of people around that could have saved her, but no one wanted to go into the dark well to get her out. When the police came, they forced someone to go in and get her, but by that time she was dead. My mom was again heartbroken; again, she lost a child.

Chapter 5

Mom, Me, and Ivan, 1950

A couple of years went by and Mom and I moved into a little house with her new boyfriend, Ivan Montana. He was short and thin with dark brown hair. He was very white with no visible signs of having African blood. Ivan was a hard worker. He went to work every day and brought food home. He took carapatti leaves, worked them and made rope to sell to bring in money; we were doing okay.

Our small, one-room house was off the main street. It was built on a little mound between two ditches that ran along side of it. During the rainy season, the ditches would fill up and divert the water away from the house. There was a bedroom, a bathroom, and a kitchen—all in this one-room house. Some people were lucky to have a beautiful house with a wooden door and a window, but we were not so lucky. In that little house, we could see if it was day or night just by looking through the cracks in the door made of the carapatti leaves. The roof was covered with these leaves also; they were kind of like banana tree leaves. We were poor with no table, so we ate on the floor. Mom and Ivan slept on an old tattered bed and I slept on the floor.

I remember the first time the molestation happened. I can remember that day as if it were today. I was about three-and-a-half years old and my mom was pregnant with my younger sister,  Zita. On that day, my mother got up very early in the morning as usual, to fix breakfast for her boyfriend to go to work. Our breakfast was made of "illa milo", toasted corn. The corn was crushed as if to make cornbread, but Mom toasted the corn first, and then crushed it.

When my mom got up to make breakfast, Ivan pointed to the bed and whispered to me, "Why don't you lay up here?" I moved up to the bed to try to be more comfortable. This was when he touched me. He quietly took me by the legs and pulled me up to his groin with my head down near his knees. He was do-

21

ing something to me that did not feel good. I turned my face toward my mother. She looked at us and saw what was happening, but looked away and then looked back in disbelief.

I wanted to say something, but for some reason, I didn't. Maybe I was too young to speak up or maybe too afraid. I was waiting for my mom to say, "What are you doing to my daughter?" But she didn't. She saw what was happening, but she didn't want to see it. She just turned her face away and kept roasting the corn.

He warned me, "Do not tell anybody what happened here today!" Maybe Mom talked to him later about it because this was the only time I can remember that Ivan abused me.

Ivan was the father of my sister Zita, and the father of my younger brother, Adrian. While Mom was still pregnant with Adrian, Ivan made plans to go to the U.S. I listened to him as he told me again, "Don't tell anybody what happened that day because I am going to the United States and I am going to send you everything I send my daughter." He told me several times that he would send to me the same as his kids. He said I was his daughter, and that I was the same as his own.

I waited a long time with anticipation to see what he would send me. I felt the most hurt when he sent the first present to Zita and Adrian and sent nothing to me. I can still remember how I felt at that age of seven. I watched to see what came out of that box, to see what was mine. But everything belonged to his children. I remember the little colored panties and the little socks with lace ruffles. They were so pretty in colors of white, pink, light blue, and yellow. There was even a pair of shiny black shoes for my sister. But for me, nothing.

I felt so betrayed; I had so much pain. I remember walking to the box, looking inside and feeling so sad, so hurt. I thought to myself, *Why did this man do this to me? He was supposed to be my daddy, my papa.* But my papa forgot about me. He didn't send anything to me like he promised. I think it was because I was not his child. This was when I started to feel sad and very lonely. I had no one in my life to love me. I was only seven and I started to feel lost. It's kind of strange and hard to explain. I would tell myself, *Someday I will get everything.*

As I grew older, I started to do more. I helped cook something we called "Manchupa", which we made with corn, "fejoa de pedra" or rock beans, and sometimes we added pork or beef, if we had some.

But because we were poor, we usually made it with just corn and beans and no meat. I also helped with making flour we called "Camoca", which was toasted corn, crushed and ground by hand until coarse or fine, depending on the purpose. It would turn kind of brown and we would add milk or coffee, or sugared cold water, or make it into an oatmeal-type mash. I did what I could to help my mom around the house to take care of the family.

I remember my mom wrote Ivan a letter and somehow I had the courage to tell her, "Ask him why he doesn't remember me." I don't know where I got the strength to ask my mom to do this, but I did and she wrote it in her letter. A few months later, lucky for me, he sent another package and this time he did send me a present. It was a little white face towel with a green stripe. I kept it for a long time because it was from him. He said he was my daddy. It made me feel so good to look at this towel, because it proved to me that he was my daddy. Though it made me feel content for a while, it also brought me a strange pain I couldn't explain. I think that if he hadn't mention to me that he was my daddy, I would have grown up not knowing what a daddy was about.

Zita was about a year and a half and Mom was pregnant with my brother, Adrian. Adrian was born in the spring of 1954; I was so proud to have a baby brother. I remember that on the 24th of June, I took him and Zita to the São João's (St. John's) Celebration where Mom had made a promise to attend. When she was about to give birth to Adrian, she made a promise to Saint John that if all went well with her pregnancy, she would participate in the walk to São João's Celebration.

I carried Adrian there and Zita followed along, clinging to my dress. I wanted to show off my little brother. I carried him with such pride, as if I were a young mother showing off her new baby. I was only seven and a half, but I felt all grown up like a little lady. There were a few women there who commented on how well I had grown up. These were the women who, as young teenagers, had fed me when I was a little crying baby. They were amazed that I had survived and was strong enough to carry a little baby myself. Then I came across our friend Nana and her neighbor, Mina. These ladies were well off because their husbands had gone to the U.S. to work and had sent them considerable amounts of money.

Nana was dressed in a beautiful long, black dress and her hair was styled up on top of her head. As she passed by me she said, "Let me see this new baby." With pride I pulled back the tattered blanket and showed her Adrian's little face. I still remember the words she used. "This baby is too ugly to be Ivan's son!"

I felt crushed. I hadn't thought of Adrian being black like me; he was just a beautiful baby to me. But to the rest of society he was black—not the color of choice. Ivan was white with dark brown curly hair. I know that Adrian is his son, but Adrian was not white like Ivan and that was too bad for him. I remember that I felt unhappy, no longer full of pride for my baby brother. We were both black and we could not change that.

I continued on my way to meet Mom at the festival house. This was the house where the food was prepared and all the festivities took place. I remember the funny plays where men were dressed up like women and we tried to guess who they were. There were also very festive musicals for us to enjoy. After these presentations the band played music for everyone to dance and I enjoyed the music and dancing the most of all.

Some people used to come from a different island called Brava to our island of Fogo. They used to bring the violin and play music. I would dance; I don't remember if they paid me to dance, because I was a good dancer. I used to enjoy dancing for them to watch me though no one knew I hid so much pain inside. I guess that when I danced, it helped kill the pain. I thought it was kind of special that people sat down to watch me dance. It was the most beautiful thing for me to do, because I liked music. I have liked it all of my life. But at the same time, I would have to ask my mom if it was okay for me to dance. I felt a little afraid that my mom might get upset with me.

A couple of miles from our house lived my

mother's best friend, Arrysa. Once in a while I would go to her house to get milk or buttermilk to bring home for my mother to feed my sister and brothers. I was the oldest in the family, but still just a very skinny little girl. I would go for a walk wearing an old ugly yellow dress with a big bucket in my hand to find something to bring home for my family to eat. There was nothing wrong with that. I was doing it to protect my family. I was helping my sister and brothers who were hungry.

One time I walked past a house that had a big testerna. The top of it was covered and it had just the one-hole opening. We would drop a bucket tied to a rope into the opening and draw out water. The house was beautiful and the owners had a lot of money. They had a dog there that I would play with when I didn't have anything else to do. It was a cute little black dog. Sometimes the dog didn't want to play with me; it was kind of a funny thing. I sat down beside it and stuck my finger in his lip; I stuck my finger in his sleepy eye; and I snapped my fingers to get him to play with me. But he continued to sleep. I got up and barked at him. He woke up and ran after me. I ran and ran and he caught up to me and bit me on the butt. I sat down and cried. I was just a little kid, maybe ten or eleven years old. I had fun with that dog except for that time when he bit me.

I would then go get the milk and return home. On the way home, the ladies in the fields picked potatoes and gave me some to give to my mom. I was always going places—other houses had beans, some houses had corn, and these women gave these things to me to give to my mom so we could have something to eat.

Chapter 6

Joãozinho Raped Me, 1956

The second molestation I can remember happened when I was nine years old. The man was white and had some mixture of black in him. He had long black hair like an Indian, but was more light-skinned. This man raped me every chance he got from the time I was nine years old until I was 18. I got pregnant at the young age of 17. It wasn't until I got pregnant that the abuse and rape stopped, but only for a couple months. For some reason the week after I had my baby, he raped me again. He left me lying on a cold, hard floor in pain, bleeding and weak. He left me to die.

Mom and I would go get firewood up in the "matto", an area kind of like low foothills with a lot of bushes. This man named Joãozinho would find a way to get me alone, away from my mom and he would rape me. He would take me down into the ditches hidden by the bushes. He covered my mouth and got whatever he wanted. His older sister knew what was going on and sometimes she saw what he did to me. She could have told him I was a helpless little girl that didn't deserve to be treated like this. She could have warned him, "Don't do it!" She could have reminded him that he already had a woman, a woman he could have anytime he wanted her. But no, she was a bitch.

She used to make fun of me. She called me a chicken and said her brother was the rooster. Nothing stopped him from being like a dog and treating me like a dog. I hate this man. I hate him so much and I hate his sister too. God, forgive me, but I hate what they put me through. I have since found Joãozinho's address. He and his sister live in Massachusetts. I'm going to write him and let him know that I remember all the awful things that he did to me. They were both ugly people, and God don't like ugly.

Chapter 7
MONSTER IN MY ROOM, 1957

After a couple of years, Ivan ordered a house to be built on some land he had from his father. The house was built of rock and it was divided into three rooms with sheets. This was around the time my mom had a little bit of money. Ivan was working in the U.S. and he sent money for my mom to take care of his kids. But things changed when Ivan got married to a woman who took over his finances. She liked to boss him around and for a while, they continued to send money, but my mom lost hope of any future with Ivan. She started to spend some of her money on dates with other guys. Other folks in the village noticed this and word got back to Ivan that my mom was going out on dates with other men. Before long, the money stopped coming. In the meantime, I had to go to other people's houses to pick beans. I didn't know how to do it, but I had to learn for us to survive.

After we moved into the big house, I sometimes walked to a place with a lot of trees. There were mango trees, papaya trees, coffee bean trees and big trees we called purgeira. People would gather the seeds from this purgeira tree to sell to make oil. It was pure oil used on people's hair or on scratches. I don't know if there are any more of these very huge trees on the island. I used to walk past these trees on my way to my friend Joanie's house, which was not too far from our house. She had two grandsons, and a little granddaughter who was too young to play with me. I didn't go there to play, but to help crush the corn, toast it, and get it ready for cooking. I didn't mind going there to work, because I liked getting out of the house.

At night, my sister and I shared a bed in one room by a window while my brother slept nearby in the same room. My sister shared the bed with me until I was around nine or ten years old, then Mom had Zita go over to sleep with Adrian and left me to sleep alone. I was confused about why my mother did this, but soon I discovered why I was to sleep alone. It was after my mom started dating other guys that the molestation started again. She worked for a big shot in town that had money and influence. I can't tell you his name and I won't dignify him with any name except Monster. For all the ugly things and pain he put me through, Monster is the only name I can call him. She started dating him and this big ugly man decided he wanted to have sex with my mom and he wanted to have sex with me too. I was only ten years old when he first raped me.

Monster came to my bed in the middle of the night. To me, as a little girl, he was a human demon. I heard this terrible voice coming from a man who was maybe 350 pounds and six foot six inches tall. He had a big belly and a big butt. I remember some of the younger guys making fun of him behind his back. They would say he had a baby in his stomach, a monkey's baby, because his belly was so big. He had a big nose and a big heavy face. He had light skin, lighter than my mother's or mine, and his hair was like that of most blacks. He was tall, he was fat, and he was ugly. At the age of ten, I began having nightmares about him. I could see this man in my dreams with his big bloody hands. All I could think of was to kill him.

One morning, thoughts of killing him kept going through my head; thoughts like poisoning him. I started to make a poison for him. I thought it had been a dream, but later on, I realized that the nightmare I had was real. I had heard that the ink on the back of Polaroid pictures was like poison, so I planned to get Monster out of my life for good.

I took some old Polaroid pictures and scraped the ink off of them and I saved it. One morning I asked Monster if he would like some coffee, and he said he did. I made him a cup and put in some of the ink scrapings from the Polaroids. I didn't want to put too much, so he wouldn't notice. He drank it down and there was no effect. The darn guy didn't die. Jesus, forgive me for trying. But let me warn you, don't try it. It doesn't work.

He'd put his hand on my mouth so I would not scream when I awoke. He didn't want the other kids to hear me and wake up. But what he and my mom didn't know was that my sister Zita sometimes was awake. When we were young, she hated me. She blamed me because she didn't understand. She thought that it was my fault that Mom's boyfriend would come to me in the night. She had no way of expressing her feelings about this connection between Monster and me, so we didn't talk about it until many, many years later. She was very mean to me when we were kids, and I think that was her way of dealing with what she didn't understand.

She often lied about me to get me in trouble. She would call me the same names that she heard my mom and the neighbors call me. She would call me, "negra, cabeca seca, minha de São Tomé", which meant black one, dry head, and little girl from São Tomé. I found out later when we spoke as adults that Monster taught her to spy on me. He gave her a gold necklace for her to catch me talking to boys. He treated her like a princess; I don't think he ever thought about molesting her. They even taught Zita to tell on me. When she got mad at me, she got a stick with these little prickly things on the end. She used the stick to scratch herself until she bled and then she would tell Mom that I beat her. No matter what I said, my mom would never believe me. Anything Zita said, they believed. My sister was stronger than I was. She ran away and grew up to be somebody. I wanted to be like that, strong and independent, but I couldn't because of my low self-esteem; because of all the things that happened to me.

My mother would slap the shit out of me to make me go to bed with her boyfriend. I still love the woman; she is my mother. At that time I had no one else. It was such a poor country. Without any money to support the family, she had to do what she had to do. But why did it have to be me? My question will always be, "Why?" Mom went back to work when I was two days old. Why couldn't she have gone back to work after my sister was born or after my brother was born? She didn't have to sell me to feed my sister and brother. I had to sell my body to a man, though I didn't want to, but I had to help support my family.

Our house was a big house. It had a stretch of land from the village street to where we lived and there were crops of sweet potatoes. Along the sides of the sweet potato plants were tall bushes of different kinds of beans. It was on the main street where everybody walked by. I liked to get outside to see people and I used to sit in the window. There were three windows—two in the front and one on the side of the house. The one on the side was where my bed was, and we divided the room. There was a room with my brothers and me, one with my sister, and one with my mom. You could see everybody's bed. There were no doors. We couldn't afford doors.

When I was in bed and everyone was asleep, I could hear this man, this big fat ugly son-of-a-bitch get out of my mom's bed and walk to where I lay. As soon as I saw him I got tears in my eyes. I knew he was coming to abuse me. I would tighten my hands between my legs and squeeze my legs together as hard as I could, but he would still do it to me.

This 350-pound monster got on top of me, a little girl of about 50 to 60 pounds. I only weighed 99 pounds when I came to the U.S. at the age of 22, so imagine how small and petite I would have been at the age of ten. Sometimes after he molested me, I got up and ran. I ran to the field and sat and hid in between the bean bushes. I would cry my heart out. I would fight and cuss; I'd scream, but not too loud because I didn't want anybody to hear me. After I was done, I would walk back to the house and not one person would ask where I had gone or what I had done. I was like nothing to them.

I got to the point that I was not sleeping because I knew he was going to wake me up. My brother was too small to do anything to protect me. It was so sad, because the people did nothing to help me. Why didn't somebody, who was an adult protect me—my mom, my aunts or uncles, somebody?

He was the one abused me, but I believe it was my mom who allowed it to happen. When I said "No" to this monster, he would grab both of my arms and hold me up against the wall and my mother would slap my face. Yes, the woman who gave me birth would force me to lie down for this ugly monster to get on top of me to do what he wanted. She is the one I blame because she empowered him by forcing me to give in to him. I believe my mom was afraid Monster would leave her for another woman if he didn't get the sex he wanted. There were a lot of things my mom made me do. There was just so much abuse, physically and mentally, that I was miserable all the time.

Chapter 8

Monster Gave Bina a Gun?

My mom's third cousin, the witch doctor, practiced witchcraft, voodoo, and black magic. He was married and he used to have a lot of teenage girls in the house to help him do his work. He would sexually abuse them. I was one of these girls. My cousin, Kathy, went there one time to hold a candle for him and she didn't like it there at all. She told her mom she didn't want to go there again. Her mom told her she didn't have to go anymore.

When I told my mom I didn't want to go there because my cousin wouldn't go, she said, "No, you are going to go!"

I don't know why my mom couldn't have been like my cousin's mom. My cousin never had to go to that place again. But me, I continued to go and sometimes I went in the dark. I didn't want anyone to see me because I was embarrassed about going there. All the other parents took their daughters out of there.

I was the only one left. I knew everyone saw what was going on. I was so sad; I was about ten years old at the time. It was this third cousin that once again ripped my innocence away. It was just too much for me to handle. Then, my life was taken over by Monster again, and I could not go anywhere. He was the one who put a stop to my going to the witchcraft cousin, but he took over the molestation.

Oh! Momma, Momma, you could have helped me! She was there. She could have helped. She could have protected me. But she didn't.

I remember being so embarrassed when I was about eleven years old. I used to pick wood in the fields to sell to make money for home. One time a man took me to bed for money. But instead of giving me money, he gave me beans mixed with corn in a little bag. I came home and gave it to my mom.

She asked, "Who gave this to you?"

I said, "Tommy." I still can remember when he was on top of me, he told me, "Your mom does it much better than you do." Goodness gracious, I was just eleven years old! What did he expect from me? But I kicked him in the balls so hard that he did not do it to me again. I don't know if he felt sorry for messing with me, but I do know he only did it once.

I still have the pain and the deep scars of the hurt that has been put upon me. But I'm not afraid anymore. I have sought relief for myself from all the pain. Writing this book was one of the ways I found to deal with the hidden pain.

I wish I had had someone I could have talked to or confided in about what was happening. Many people knew what was going on. There were people besides my mother who knew. I'm not talking about my aunt and uncle, who lived far from us, but I'm sure they heard about it. I had one aunt who lived nearby, but she didn't have much voice either. She was poor with a bunch of kids from different fathers, but I knew she loved me. She was there for me. I was so afraid of my mother that I couldn't open my mouth to say anything to anybody. I know she knows some of the men who abused me, because she allowed them to. But some of them, she didn't know because I didn't tell her. I know one thing, when I went out to look for work at the age of eleven, I brought home five dollars. I brought beans, potatoes, squash, and milk. I helped provide for the family; I did my share, but I can't say that I was loved for doing it.

My mom became pregnant with my baby brother, Fernando, from one of the guys she dated. Fernando's father, Nuno, never touched me. He felt sorry about what was happening to me.

Chapter 9
Maybe Angola, 1959

When I was about 12 years old, my mom wanted to let this lady, Mrs. Cabral, adopt me to take me to Angola. But I'm so glad my mom didn't let her take me, because I might have been killed there like so many others. Or, who knows? I might have survived, I don't know. I'm not quite sure of how it all happened, but the best I can recall was I overheard them talking.

Mrs. Cabral told my mom, "If you want me to take Bina to Angola, I can adopt her. I can only take her if you let me adopt her." She had a husband and several kids, and she was willing to make me part of her family.

I looked at my mom and she said, "Yeah, you can talk to the people, and find out if we can do that." In one way I wanted to go, to get out of the situation I was in, the rape and stuff. But on the other hand I thought, *My God, my mom doesn't want me! What did I do that was so bad that my mom doesn't want me? She'd been letting those guys rape me every day. She didn't care about me and now she wanted to send me to Angola! They kill people in Angola!* From what I heard, many people from our islands were going to Angola, because the whites had kind of brainwashed them. Many of my people got beat up, they were abused and almost half of those who went were killed. No, I didn't want the life I was living, but I didn't want to die either. Mrs. Cabral never did adopt me, and she and her family went to Angola without me.

There was this time I went with my friends to get water from a "ribeira", which is like a ditch. We retrieved water there because sometimes it was the only way to get water. We took the water home to use for drinking, cooking, and cleaning. We didn't take baths, but we would put water in a bucket to wash ourselves. We would also take a wash basin and our dirty clothes to the ribeira and wash them there. Some women got paid to wash other people's clothes; they would spend the whole day at the ribeira washing clothes. It was a wonderful time for me because I liked to get out of the house. It gave me the chance to play along the way with my friends, with other teenage kids.

On the way to get water, we used to play, hold hands, and twirl each other around and around. One time I got so dizzy that I fell and broke my arm. That day we stayed too long and my mom was already on her way to look for us—my cousin, the other girls, and me. My arm was broken and I had a makeshift sling wrapped around my neck with my arm in it. My mom was so upset that she really beat my ass. Even with my broken arm, she didn't give a damn. This made it hard for me to lift my right hand to my head to do the sign of the cross, to give grace after meals. I would use my left hand to hold up my right hand, because it was very heavy. It was awhile before I got to go wash clothes again.

While growing up in my teens, my cousin, Sonya Maria, was the same age as me and there was one other girl named Lydia. I think Lydia was a couple of years older. Where I lived there weren't many houses. But then Sonya Maria and Lydia's families left with a lot of the other young people I knew. It became an even emptier place. It was a very sad time in my life; I felt I was left there alone. It was around the time I was being raped. I had no friend to confide in. It was like they took all those people to Angola.

There was a war going on and I didn't know exactly what the war was about. Everybody wanted to go because it was supposed to be a better life there, a better situation. Some of them went and had a better life with a good education, I was not lucky enough to have someone take me, not Mrs. Cabral, not anyone.

I remember very clearly, one of the men who kissed Monster's ass was Maneé. He was one of the more important men in the village. Maneé was like a policeman of our village. He looked at me and said,

"Hi! How are you doing?" It seemed he was trying to get me to talk to him about the things he already knew were going on, but I just could not talk. I had the feeling that he wasn't going to help me anyhow. He liked to come over when my mother wasn't home and give me candy. He would give me things that I could eat really fast. Once he came by and gave me a little red apple. At that time in my country, I heard that if a man gave a woman a red apple it meant that he loved the woman. So, during this time he kept playing with me, teasing me, leading me on until he got me.

He came by another time and gave me a little red flower, a carnation, but I had to throw it away before my mom got home. I thought he was just being nice to me, but in reality, he was just trying to gain my confidence so he could do what he wanted to me. I already had low self-esteem; I already believed I was ugly; I thought no one was going to want me and no one was going to love me. That's all I had ever heard. Of course, this man buttered me up and had me feeling good so he could get me anytime he wanted to.

He started flirting with me and taking advantage of me when I was 12. It got to the point that when I saw him, I would try to run and hide somewhere. But where was I going to hide on that little island? I couldn't scream, because if I screamed, no one wanted to hear me.

Chapter 10
VOODOO KILLS, 1959

This is a story about witchcraft. I had a cousin named Delida, whom I met when I was about 11 or 12 years old and she was around 35 to 40 years old. She was the most beautiful lady—light skinned, and beautiful black hair. She was a lady who had a pretty good life. She had a beautiful house, she had money, and she had a lot of gold. But because of witchcraft, everything was going little by little. She was dying from witchcraft. Someone put a Voodoo spell on her using a cockroach. She had a live cockroach in her body, crawling under skin. It ate her skin. She had to lie in a bed and couldn't do anything for herself. Delida had two sons. One of them was in Portugal studying in college. He had heard how bad his mom was doing, so he was on his way from Portugal to the Cape Verde Islands to take care of her.

His mother was crying, praying out loud, "God, help me to see my son one more time!" It was around that time that we went to visit her. My mom's witch doctor cousin, who was also a cousin of Delida, his wife, and another couple went with us to see if there was any way to help her.

But I saw when Nenné got there and looked at Delida, he said, "I can't help her. We waited too long; there is nothing I can do for her."

Delida died three days later. We came to find out that the people who did the witchcraft voodoo to her were—guess? It was her housekeepers. They took everything she owned: her gold, her clothes, and all the furniture. We really believed in witchcraft in those days. But now, I believe in God more than witchcraft, because I know God is higher and more powerful than anything in the world. But sometimes I wonder why a lot of things happen. I believe in God, but sometimes I wonder where God is. Why didn't Delida get to see her son? Why?

***

I was a kid when my uncle got really sick. Uncle Alfredo had a few girlfriends. He was a player like most men were. He asked one of the girlfriends to marry him, but then a couple of months later, he changed his mind. He got another girlfriend to move in with him. He then started to get sick. No matter what he ate, whatever he put in would have to come right back out. He could not work; he couldn't do anything.

Uncle Alfredo went to the doctor but even he wasn't much help. We didn't have many doctors. The few we had made all kinds of medication, but nothing seemed to cure my uncle. He didn't want to believe anything about Voodoo.

His and my mother's cousin, Nenné, sent Uncle Alfredo a message that said, "You need to come get medication from me."

Uncle Alfredo said, "No, I don't believe in that kind of stuff."

He asked, "Which do you believe—that you are going to die or that you can get cured? What you have is not from God."

My mother asked me to go there to help her cousin to do the work to cure her brother. I was afraid, but I was kind of excited at the same time, because I wanted to know what was going on, and how they were going to reverse the Voodoo. What I saw was that there are a lot of things involved in doing Voodoo. I cannot go into details about what happened, or how it was done, but the young man, who was my mom's cousin, did cure my uncle by using some black magic. I did whatever I could to help my uncle, but I cannot discuss it in this book.

***

There was a very nice, beautiful young lady named Luciana who found herself a nice boyfriend. His name was Stephan. After they had gotten to know each other, they fell in love and six months later they made arrangements to get married. Stephan other girlfriends before he met Luciana. One of these old girlfriends was very jealous of her. I didn't like the way she looked at Luciana, but there was nothing I could do about it. The day before the wedding, the old girlfriend gave Luciana an apple. She ate it and she got very sick. The day of the wedding Luciana had so much pain. It was so sad.

Her fiancé cried, "Don't die on me, please don't die on me!" Her fiancé didn't know what to do. He took her to the local clinic, but she didn't make it. Later on, the old girlfriend said she was the one who brought the apple to the house. She bragged about how she put a Voodoo spell on it. It was sad, but it happened. There are a lot of evil people in this world. It's true; it was Voodoo. She was the one who admitted it. She was jealous and evil, and she turned to Voodoo.

***

In the middle of being awake and asleep is when I would see this lady with big eye shadow makeup the color of deep green. I think of her as the Lima Bean Lady. She was fat and tall, but her legs were so skinny—skinnier than my arm. She wanted to make me eat lima beans and that was one thing I didn't like to eat. In my conscious/unconscious state, she forced me to eat the beans; she stuck them in my mouth with no salt or seasoning. Maybe that's the reason that I still don't like lima beans. When I ate the beans, the lady disappeared. I couldn't tell anybody about the lady. She took me to the top of a hill and tried to push me down into the ditch, but I always saved myself from dying. For some reason, God was good to me on the other side of that hill, and I always helped myself. I really believe in God, but again sometimes, I wonder where he is.

There was this man in our neighborhood that went out of his mind. He screamed once and after that he just made noises from his nose. When his parents found out, they took him to the hospital. The man was unable to walk, so it took four men to carry him. They had to carry him because where we lived there were no cars and no transportation. When they passed by my house, the man was in terrible pain. At the hospital the man was pronounced dead. He was only 22 years old. The Lima Bean Lady was the one who killed this man. I kept seeing her for years, but I never shared that with anybody. When I was a kid, I couldn't talk. Maybe that's the reason why I talk too much today!

Voodoo kills. Voodoo does kill.

Chapter 11
LIED ABOUT UNCLE JOSÉ, 1960

My mom had a friend named Campanha who got married in the village. Our family was invited, but Mom and Monster didn't want to go. My Uncle José asked my mom if he could take me along to keep his daughter company. Mom said okay and I went with my cousin, Ria, and my Uncle José to the wedding. Though I only had a raggedy old dress to wear, I still had a good time.

About a month later, the newlyweds moved right across the street from where we lived. At the time, we were living a little better; we were able to butcher a pig to have meat for the year. Mom salted the meat and saved it in a container. One day the new bride passed by our house and stopped in to visit. I was by myself as usual and she asked me if I could give her a piece of meat to cook for their dinner. I did give her the meat, but later I wondered if Monster had put her up to this task just to start something. When the new husband came home and she had the pork dinner ready, he asked her where she got the meat.

She replied, "Bina gave it to me."

He asked, "Why would Bina give you this meat? What did you do for Bina?"

The wife answered, "I caught Bina with her Uncle José in bed together. Bina then paid me with this meat so I wouldn't tell on her." It was after this incident that the rumors started around the village about Uncle José and me. I really think Monster put her up to say this lie. He wanted trouble for my Uncle José. He wanted him out of our lives because my uncle was very suspicious of Monster molesting me.

As the rumors became more gossip, Mom and Monster told me to say that my uncle had touched me inappropriately. I was only a 14-year-old girl who was afraid of them. My mom said she would beat me unless I did what I was told. Monster offered me a gold necklace, gold earrings and a new pair of shoes. I had never had a pair of shoes and this would be my first pair. Monster convinced the judge's wife, Daisy, to offer me a new dress.

Daisy would make a new dress for me to wear to my cousin's wedding if I would say that my uncle touched me. She even asked me, "What color of dress do you want?" I said I wanted a black skirt and a white top. I only had two raggedy old dresses and no shoes. Having been poor all of my life, as a teenager all these things they offered me were just too overwhelming to let go. I was so excited to hear I was going to get the necklace, the earrings, the new pair of shoes and the dress, but deep inside I felt bad. I liked my Uncle José. I liked to stand behind him and play with his soft dark brown hair. I didn't want to lie about him. I didn't want him to get into trouble, but if I didn't do what they said, Mom would beat me and I wouldn't get any of those nice things.

The judge's house had a store in one room and in another room was where the village conflicts and disputes where settled. Mom, Monster, and Daisy met in a third room, a little room to the side, where they talked to me to convince me to lie. When it came time to talk to the judge, I could not look at my Uncle José. The judge asked me if my uncle had touched me inappropriately.

I lied and said, "Yes, he touched me." I felt so guilty. That evening I went to spend the night at my mom's sister's house. No one would talk to me, and that was very unusual. Everyone in the family was upset with me. It made me feel even worse.

My Aunt's husband went out the next morning to milk his cows. I hadn't slept much all night, and when I heard him going out, I ran after him. I called, "Tio Arturo, it's not true!"

He said, "What?"

I said, "I lied about Uncle José. He never touched me."

Tio Arturo replied, "If he never touched you, and you lied against him, you need to go to church and ask for forgiveness." He continued to walk to his destination. I didn't know what he meant at that time. I turned back to the house, feeling very sad and lonely. I knew I had done wrong, lying about my uncle, but I had no other choice. One way or another, I was going to be in trouble.

Chapter 12

BINA'S LIFE AS A TEENAGER, 1962-64

ROY

I don't know if they still have the special festival dance in my country, but a long time ago during the time of celebrating Saint's Day, the island people would make a special kind of candy called dropes. They made this candy bar out of sweet milk, coconut, and nuts. I really liked these and I also liked other sweets called asuccarinha and reposados.

At the time, I was a teenager and in love with an older man. He was about 22 years old and was my first love. Roy was the only man who respected me and treated me like I was a young lady and not a kid. He never once abused me or tried to use me; he is the only man that I ever considered to be my boyfriend. Roy knew about all the abuse that was happening to me.

Roy had a younger sister. She used to take dropes candies to the local festival dance. Roy told her, "Go give Bina as much candy as she wants. She can split it with her friends."

His sister was so suave; I liked the girl a lot. She came to me and told me, "Bina, pick all the candy you want and share it with your friends!" Right after she came and told me this, I looked up at my mom to see if she was watching me, and she was. She looked me dead in the eye to make sure I did not take the candy. I was so scared of my mother that I did not dare take it.

My mother never let me have any candy. I was around 15 years old; it was not like I was a baby. She didn't like to see me have anything that would make me happy and I could not dance with anybody but Monster. These were my mother's rules. She was there watching me like a hawk. I was not supposed to look or smile at any boys, especially not Roy. My mother hated Roy. She would have my sister spy on me, and any time Zita saw me with Roy she would go back and tell her and Monster.

On the evening of April 25th, while we attended the St. Felipe celebration dance, Monster requested for the music to be stopped and for an announcement to be made. Right there out on the dance floor the man announced, "Bina cannot dance with Roy!" I remember back to a time when my uncle would make a distraction for my mother and Monster, so that Roy and I could dance together.

Roy stepped out on the dance floor and declared, "If Bina cannot dance with Roy, then Bina is not going to dance with anyone else." Yahoo! I loved it, I loved it. He was my man. I loved that part.

Roy was handsome. He had dark skin like me and his body was thick with muscles, no fat. He had a good-looking full head of black hair and very dark eyes. He liked to dress in black pants with a blue or white shirt that fit him perfectly. He was so clean, looked so good, and dressed so well, that I couldn't help but fall in love with him. Everybody got quiet, because he was very stern, strong and a very good fighter. He would never bother anybody, but if somebody bothered him, he could take care of himself.

The men, who were in charge of making the announcement, were men who already did not like Roy because Monster had a lot of influence in the village. Monster's uncle had a lot of money but had no children, and Monster was his only nephew. Because we lived in a poor country, the villagers kissed this man's ass and sided with him against other people. It was so unfair. There were so many other women there, why did Monster have to pick me? I was only a child. Besides, Monster was my mom's man, her boyfriend, not my man. What was the matter with those people? Lord, have mercy. They all sided with Monster, no matter how wrong it was.

This was like some of the situations I saw on the TV. When I saw these TV shows, it reminded me of a lot of things. The difference was that I didn't fight and I didn't want to have those things happening to me. It's the worst thing that could happen to anyone. It's not because I liked it; it's because I had no choice.

After Roy's announcement, my mother grabbed my hand and said, "Let's go home!" I had to leave with the rest of the family. I cried so hard because I didn't get to go dancing very often and here was another lost opportunity. I loved to dance and I loved to get out of the house.

This was the cruel teenage life I had. I wouldn't wish this on anyone. I had so much respect for Roy. I still love the man, even though we never kissed each other on the lips. Each time he talked to me, he told me things of my past that I didn't remember. I guess I was so young that I couldn't remember, but it made me love him even more. It showed me how much respect this man had for me. He could not touch me sexually while knowing all the ugly things that had happened to me. So he held my hand, he gave me hugs; he kissed me on the forehead and on the cheek. He rubbed my shoulders and then he would just look at me.

When I looked into his eyes, it looked like he wanted to cry. He was sad. I didn't understand. I was confused. It does make me feel happy to have had this kind of person who respected me and loved me so much that he thought of my feelings before his. But I often wondered why he didn't take me out of the situation that I was in. Now, I know why. He didn't have any power. The way that my family didn't like him, the way they were all against him; they could have put him in jail because I was only 15 years old. It was so sad that they were against this man, and soon I had to let Roy go. My mother was never going to allow us to be happy together.

Roy would have been the best thing for me for the rest of my life. And then in late 1964 I met Roy's cousin, Armando. Armando introduced himself to my mother and me, and my mother already began making plans in her mind for us. She liked Armando, and she believed that he was going to be the perfect man for me. So, Armando and I began seeing one another.

Armando was tall and thin with brown skin and curly hair. He had a raspy sounding voice. I didn't love Armando; I just kind of liked him. I guess I liked him enough to do anything to get out of the situation that I was in at home. I tried to love him, but after I was three months pregnant with my first child, Armando started seeing another woman. He didn't want his sister to know he had a kid on the way.

Three more months passed and as I was close to seven months pregnant, he left me and married another woman. The day of the wedding he thought it would be funny to go in the opposite direction of his home and pass by my home with the celebration, music, people, and fireworks. And with all that it just made me feel worse. It wasn't just him but his wife too; his wife made him do it. After he got married to this woman, he felt so sorry about what he did. He used to run after me. I still waited and hoped that Roy would come back to get me.

I thought to myself, *Now that I'm pregnant, I hope that Roy will take me this way.* I also wondered if now my mom would let me go with Roy. Roy sent me a message through our friends that if I still wanted to be with him that he would be waiting for me. Now I don't know how my mother knew, but she did.

He came by our house and threw rocks at the window and my mom heard it. She opened the house door, looked at me and said, "BITCH, if you want to go, the door is open!"

I was so scared that I pretended to be asleep; my mom would beat me up even if I was pregnant, I just knew it. My Godmother liked Roy very much. She told me if I wanted to marry Roy, I should move in with her and she would marry me to him just like she was my mom. I think she may have known about the molestation because she told me this over and over. I was so afraid of my mom that I just couldn't. Every time I saw my mom my body froze, almost like I was looking the devil in his face.

I got to the point that I knew I could not do anything with Roy. One night I got on my knees and prayed that God would take my mind from Roy, and from that moment on I stopped thinking about him. On January 6, 1965, I gave birth to my first child, a baby boy I call Manny—my first real love.

On this particular winter day in January, 1965, I was in a lot of pain because I had just had my baby boy. He was a cute baby, though black like me. His father didn't have anything to do with him, and would not even support him. It was three days after Manny was born that my mom was out with my brothers and sister. This man that had molested me from the time I was nine years old, came to the house. He had raped me countless times through the years and he was there again to take advantage of me.

When I saw this man walk in the door, I called his name, "Joãozinho!" and I said, "Please, don't do this because I'm hurt and I'm in a lot of pain!" He didn't listen to me; he did it anyway. He raped me three days after I had my first child. I still feel the pain. He left me there on the floor. I thought I was going to pass out. My baby was crying; I was crying. I was losing so much blood. This man Joãozinho was heartless; he didn't even look back to see if I was okay. He always got away with it.

Chapter 13

FIRST MARRIAGE, 1965

Six months later, I had a strange guest come over to my house. His name was José and he lived in a village about two hours away from us. I did not know this man, but my mother did. I had just gotten news that I had permission to go to the United States. Now this man whom I had never seen before asked me to marry him. I was in disbelief.

I was one of the very few who had permission to go to the U.S. I should have been able to marry the man I wanted, but because of my mother, I did not have a choice—not as a child, and now not as an adult choosing my marriage partner. Sometimes I stop myself and wonder what is wrong. It took me a little while to figure this out. I didn't even know the concept of having a choice. When I was growing up, I had been taught to always respect and obey my parents, all adults, and that I was supposed to do whatever a man said. They just opened their mouth and they had me.

He said, "My name is José Cana and I have heard that you are going to the U.S. I will marry your daughter and take care of her for you. And when she goes to the U.S., I will pay her way and mine." My mother didn't ask me for my opinion, or if it was all right or not. She had a daughter with a baby and she needed someone to take care of me while she went to the U.S. I was 18 1/2, and at the age to be married off. Nothing I could say would change anything, and I didn't want to make my mom mad. So I left my village of Talia and moved to José Cana's village of Cazinha. I was to live with José and his family until the day we would get married.

When I got to his village, I noticed the area was like a desert with mountains, coffee, papaya, and mango trees. It was a little village that did not have many houses. There was one rich family from Lisbon, Portugal who owned a big ranch. They also owned all the workers' houses in that area. The people who lived in the small houses took care of the ranch and the main house. The owner's house had a good sturdy roof on it and there was a water wheel in the front of the house. My husband and his family lived in the guesthouse.

It was a very poor little place for us to live, where I was to stay with José, who was between 38 and 42 years old. He had a son who was 13 years old and he had a niece. I had my six-month-old son with me, who meant nothing to José. It was a really sad time for me because I had no feelings for this man.

José was looking for someone to bring him to the United States. My mom gave me away and this was one of the reasons I was most upset with her. I should not have had to marry someone I did not love just to please her. But on October 13, 1965, we went to the church to get married. It was one of the saddest days of my life. We had no car, so we walked. I left the house early before he did and I walked two blocks ahead of him to the church. We did not look like a couple going to church to get married. After we got there, I stood in the dress my cousin had traded with me. She liked one of my dresses and I liked this dress that was white with green flowery straps.

I just stood there when the Father asked three times during the ceremony if I would accept this man as my husband. I could not say yes. With tears in my eyes I thought, *If I do not do this, I will not see my mom anymore.* I had no family there to support me at church or in the village; I didn't know anyone. After we were married, we walked back home. I walked ahead of him again. My mother-in-law had made some homemade chicken soup for everyone. That was our wedding celebration. We had no cake, no music, no gifts—it was not a celebration for me. This marriage meant nothing to me.

At that time, my husband had three girlfriends. None of his girlfriends lived with him. He lived with his mother, grandmother, his son, and his niece. His niece was 10 or 11 years old. His mother didn't like me because I was black. She was a white woman, but her son's skin was the same color as mine. His mom did the cooking, but I had to prepare the corn meal. I would get up early, like 3:00 or 4:00 in the morning to beat the corn to make it into corn meal ready for her to cook. When one of my husband's girlfriends passed by the house to let my mother-n-law know they were going to town, I had to have the corn ready for my mother-in-law to cook. This was because the girlfriend stopped by to eat with them. One night, one of the girlfriends was allowed to spend the night with my husband. Everyone in the neighborhood knew this woman was spending the night. That night, I was not allowed to sleep in our bed. I was told to sleep on the floor because the girlfriend was to sleep with my husband. When the girlfriend was there, I slept on a blanket called "mistera" made of "cankara" which is like bamboo. This was the poor African way to sleep—it was as low as you could go to sleep on the floor. My husband and my mother-in-law both warned me about the bed, that I was to sleep on the floor. This happened on my wedding day.

The girlfriend was the mother of José's 13-year-old son. Again, I had to get up very early in the morning to prepare the corn meal to fix the food for this woman to eat who was sleeping with my husband. I couldn't talk to anyone about this. Even today, my sister does not know this, my brother does not know this, and my cousin does not know that I was sleeping on the floor while other women slept with my husband.

My mother-in-law would wake me early every day, just in case people passed by. She didn't want them to catch me sleeping on the floor because everything was supposed to be private; no one was supposed to know. Then came the day that I overslept. This man walked by and he saw me pick up my mistera and my bamboo bed off of the floor.

He leaned back and said, "Bina, good morning. You sleep on the floor?" I was so embarrassed, that I kept walking. I didn't talk to him, because I didn't want him to know. I didn't want anyone to know. I don't know why; I guess I just believed that there was no one there to help me.

This man went home to talk to his wife. He told his wife, "I think Bina has been sleeping on the floor."

We had no phones at that time, so we just shouted to get each other's attention. Their house was not too far behind ours. When his wife saw me outside, she called out, "Bina," and I turned around and looked at her and she continued, "Meet me halfway, I want to talk to you." When I met her, she said, "Bina, don't do it. Don't sleep on the floor to let somebody else sleep with your husband. If you guys love each other or not, he is still your husband. You deserve the respect. If it happens again that you have to sleep on the floor, you come to sleep in my house. I have a bed for you."

I felt good, because she was the first person who talked to me like that. It kept happening. I was forced to sleep on the floor each time that girlfriend came over to be with my husband, and there were other women also. But when that lady called me and said, "It's enough," I made up my mind and I just started spending the night over at her house.

One of our neighbors had a better life. He was a young, attractive man named Aledio. He had a girlfriend. His sister was like a housekeeper to help around the house. I believe I was set up.

One day, my neighbor's sister came to me and said, "Bina, you know my brother likes you?" I was a very young 18, and I guess my mind was more like a 10-year-old. The neighbor's sister said, "Why don't you date my brother?"

I said, "Because I am married."

She said, "So, what?" One day she came to me and said, "My brother wants to meet you at such and such a place.

I said, "No, I can't do that."

She asked, "Can't you see how your mother-in-law treats you?"

I just let it go. About three weeks went by and my husband's girlfriend came more often to the house. There was nothing I could do about that. What really upset me was the way that my mother-in-law treated me.

I continued to prepare the corn and when my mother-in-law made the meal for lunch or dinner, she put the food on a plate and slid it across the floor saying, "Bina, this is yours." But the girlfriend would get served special, like she was a princess or something. I had to sit there and watch all that.

So, I decided to meet this man. Maybe he would be someone who would love me. When the time came to meet with him, my husband already knew I was to meet him because the sister had told him. He was a nice, tall, good-looking young man. I thought to myself, *Here is a man I would like to be with.*

When I left the house it was not far, just across the street. Even though I didn't really love my husband, I still didn't want to see him sleeping with another woman while I was there on the floor. That was cruel to make me go through that embarrassment. It was around 9:00 in the evening and kind of dark. We met, and he started to kiss me. I was so unhappy at home that I was ready to let him do anything. My husband knew exactly where we were and grabbed my hand and pushed me. I fell, hitting my head on a rock. I cut my head really badly and blood was everywhere.

The next morning my mother-in-law told my husband, "You have to take her to the clinic." It was about a four-hour walk, but he refused to take me because he was mad. I didn't blame him, because he caught me with another man.

I had to walk by myself. I left about 5:00 in the morning and I was soaked in blood. My friend, Rosy, who I knew before I was married, asked how I got hurt. I told her that I tripped and fell. I never told her the truth. I wanted everyone to think everything was okay. The doctor put six or seven stitches in my head and when he was done, I walked back home.

The young man had followed me. He rode over to my husband's house on a horse. I was embarrassed to see him because I really did not want to do it with him, but I was mad and I wanted revenge because I wanted attention.

I stared at the ground, and he said to me, "Bina, if you are not happy, I can get you another home. I will take care of you."

I said, "No! You leave me alone!" But because he lived so close, I saw him every day. He had more power than my husband, so my husband could not do anything to him. This young man gave me $100. I think he felt sorry for me. I don't think he knew it was a set up. After he offered me some nice things, I thought that maybe this man really did like me. But I could not leave my husband, because my mom would kill me.

This young man's girlfriend was white and very pretty with long, brown hair. He used to beat her up. I was afraid he would beat me up also, so this was one reason I would not accept his offer. After he gave me the money, he took me to the clinic. He talked to the doctor and told him he was my neighbor. He told them if there was anything I needed, to let him know. Everyone knew who he was. He talked to his cousin there and asked her if I could stay with her so I wouldn't have to walk the four hours back home. I stayed there with his cousin for three days.

I had one aunt and one uncle who were my mother's siblings. They were the only ones in my family who would support me, but they lived too far away. The news about my husband finding out about my affair got to my mom in the U.S. It was a big thing, especially on my island. If your husband catches you having an affair—my God you didn't do these things. I was so embarrassed when I got back home, I just wanted to die. The sister and his girlfriend looked at me and laughed.

The sleeping on the floor got worse. I moved my bamboo mattress to the room where the other women slept—my mother-in-law and her mom. I had a very small space, but then again, I really didn't take up much space.

I worked like a slave picking beans and collecting firewood. We lived in a house that was off the main street and when I worked, I had no one to watch my baby boy. From the house to the main street was a rock pathway where my son sometimes crawled and scraped his knees. When he fell and scraped his knees, no one would pick him up when he cried.

One day my son's grandfather passed by and heard him crying. His grandfather picked him up and waited for me to come home. When I got home, he was in the hallway waiting for me with Manny sitting on his lap. He said, "Bina, I'm going to take Manny with me."

I took a deep breath. I didn't like the idea, because I knew that I would miss him. But I also knew I didn't have any other choice. He suffered the same fate I did. I worked and had no one to take care of him just like my mom had no one to take care of me. When he was hungry or dirty and he cried, no one picked him up until I got home from work. My husband's family did not help me with my son at all.

Manny was about two years old when his grandfather came by the house to see him. He saw how they treated him. I gave my son to him because I knew he was suffering. His grandparents lived on a different island called Brava.

I went to visit my son at least three times a year before I came to live in the U.S. It took me about a year working in Massachusetts to raise enough money to send for Manny. By the end of 1970, he was with me again.

Chapter 14

Lalo in San Felipe, 1965

I very sick with appendicitis and needed to go to the hospital. It was while I was in the hospital that my mom took a ship to the United States. The hospital was in San Felipe, a large ocean-port town. From my hospital room window, I could see all the ships coming and going. When my mother's ship left port, my mom asked them to put the white flag up that stood for "goodbye" and to blow the ship horn for me. I cried and cried. I was so sick and in so much pain. I stayed in the hospital for a week. I did not have one person visit me while I was there. I was in a room with a woman named Marianna who was about 45 years old. Her daughter lived nearby and when she would come to visit her mom and bring her food, she would bring me some too.

A week later I checked out of the hospital to come back to my miserable home. It was much better in the hospital than at home. I had no one to pick me up. I had to walk from San Felipe back to my town, Cazinha. I had to walk slowly, so it took me more than two days. It was hot during the day and I had no shoes on. I arrived at the village of Pico at about 10:00 at night. I could not see to walk anywhere. I stopped at the house of Zita and Adrian's godmother and knocked on her door.

When she opened the door she asked, "Who are you?"

I said, "I am Linda's daughter. Can I spend the night here with you until tomorrow? I'm so tired, hungry, and thirsty."

She looked at my face and saw the tears and said, "Yes, yes come in." She was pretty well off. She had a house complete with furniture and a housekeeper. She called the housekeeper and said to me, "What's your name, again?"

I said, "Bina."

She told the housekeeper, "Bring something for Bina to eat." I ate a little, but I was so tired I just wanted to lie down and rest. The next morning when I got up, she gave me breakfast of bread and coffee and some food to eat for my trip home. It took me another day's walk to get home. I spent the next night at a couple's house about two hours from my town. They knew my mother. The town was Campanas. The next day I started walking home.

When my mother-in-law saw me walking, she tossed her head back and said, "Hum, she is here now." No one asked me how the surgery went, or how I felt.

One month after my surgery, I had an appointment to go back for a checkup with the doctors. There was a friend of my mom's who lived 20 minutes from downtown San Felipe. I walked to her house and spent my first night there before continuing on to the hospital the next morning. On my way to San Felipe, a strong, handsome young man approached me on a motorcycle and asked me where I was going. I told him I was headed for the hospital. He said he would give me a ride there, so I hopped on the back of his motorcycle and we rode to the hospital. When he dropped me off he said, "I'll pick you up later." I felt good because I had someone do something nice for me.

Later when the young man came by to pick me up, one of the nurses said to him, "Oh, no. Bina is going to my house. We'll see you later, Lalo." I came to find out that this nurse named Gina was a cousin to my husband. Gina and her sister, Violet, lived like most of the rich people on the island, in this big town of San Felipe.

My husband never mentioned these cousins. Gina was a nurse at the hospital and Violet was a teacher at one of the local schools. They wore nice dresses, high heels, and perfume. They were classy people. I went home with Gina that evening. We washed up and had dinner. Violet was glad to meet me, and asked about my husband. They wanted to take me out, but I had no nice clothes and no shoes to wear. Gina was a little plump, but she took some of her clothes in so that they would fit me. She let me borrow a pair of her shoes and we went out.

I started feeling very comfortable around them. They were like people who lived in the U.S. It was like nothing I had ever known. They invited me to stay and every evening after dinner we would go for a walk in the gardens. They had beautiful lights and flowers, and it was very romantic. The ladies taught me how to wear makeup, lipstick, and how to style my hair. They were both married to rich old men who were always away on business. I had a good time with them. I stayed with them for over two months. No one ever came to look for me. I guess no one cared if I was gone from home.

The sisters took me to watch a soccer game. I had never seen soccer before. The girls fooled around on their husbands and both of their boyfriends were at the soccer game. Gina and Violet wanted to hook me up with Lalo, the guy with the motorcycle. Lalo's father owned some stores in town and a big ship named *Stina* which traveled around the world. Lalo was good looking and a good soccer player. I had a crush on him. I liked the way his legs looked—so muscular from playing ball.

When he rode his motorcycle by my friends' house, he pulled over and said, "Come on, let me give you a ride." He told me to hold on real tight. We drove all over town, talking, stopping for ice cream and refreshments. I felt good then; I was happy. There was no hanky-panky going on between us. We would laugh and talk and I was happy. He drove me back home to my husband's cousins' house.

We met one more time at the gardens and we talked. I told him I had to go back to my town the next day. I was sad. I really didn't want to return to my miserable home. The last time I saw Lalo was when I boarded ship to come to the U.S. I saw him and I said good-bye once more. It was a little hard to let go of the wonderful times we shared. Later I heard that he had come to the United States, but I never saw him again. I often think about him. He was a good friend. He was a good person, handsome, and rich. Unfortunately for me, I was married and I could not make Lalo a part of my life.

Chapter 15

BINA BECOMES SWOLLEN

Like I said, I was married at 18 years old and I moved to the other part of the island. It was all strange people; I didn't know anybody there. I felt even my husband was strange. I never cared to marry him, I never loved him, but we were husband and wife. Things got very ugly. I knew a few things about Voodoo, but I didn't know that people could do Voodoo to me. I never had concern to do anything bad to anybody. At 18, I was no kid, but in my mind I was very naïve.

My mother was in the United States and had sent me some clothes—nice dresses, and nice things to wear. Even after all I had been through, I had a nice body. I had a beautiful shape; I was about a size 3 or a size 5. Around the time that I received these clothes, I started to get sick every morning from 10:00 until at least 7:00 at night. I became swollen from my feet to my head. I couldn't wear anything. All the nice things I got, I could not wear because I was so swollen. I didn't throw up, I didn't get dizzy; I didn't have any pain, but I swelled up all over. The only thing I could wear was a bed sheet. I made a hole in the sheet to stick my head in and the rest of the sheet went all the way to the ground. That's what I wore during the day. At night, the swelling would go away, I felt good and I went back to my original size. I could wear my nice clothes, but it was time for me to go to sleep.

My mother-in-law said that something was not right. They were going to find a way to help me out because she wanted her son to go to the United States. That was what the marriage was about. My mother-in-law looked for somebody like a witchdoctor, to take the Voodoo from me because they already knew that there was no way for me to get sick like that.

The place we went to find the cure was far away. We walked for a good four to five hours to get to there. When I got there to see the lady, she cured me and gave me some herbs. She told me where someone had lit a candle with my name on it. This candle was in a place where I passed by to go home. The lady told me to go straight home, but I stopped by that place and got the candle and took it home with me. When I got home my mother-in-law said, "No, you shouldn't touch this; you might get worse."

She was right; I became even sicker. It was about midnight and I left the house and walked from the village of Cazinha to my village of Talia. I knocked on the door of my aunt's house at 2:00 in the morning.

When my aunt saw me she screamed, "Oh my child, what is wrong with you?"

I couldn't explain to her what was going on or why I was there because I didn't even know I was going there. I left home and I didn't know I was walking until I got to my aunt's house. It was when I knocked on the door and she answered and screamed that I realized where I was. Yes, it was Voodoo. I don't remember if I lost my mind a little bit but I do remember my uncle went to the other part of the island to get the medicine for me because I was out of my mind.

I believe one of my husband's girlfriends who practiced Voodoo put a spell on me so I would die before I went to the United States. But you know, God loved me, and I love God.

I do remember when my Uncle Joe went to get the herbs because we did not have those herbs where we were. He asked for me to go spend the night with my cousin, his daughter. It was a full moon and the moon was so clear. I was 18 to 19 years old, between 1965 and 1966. My aunt boiled the herbs in a bucket so I could sit down in it to take a bath. We didn't have bathtubs at that time. When I smelled the herbs, I sneaked out and ran. I ran from the house at midnight. That was the time the doctor told my uncle I had to take the herb bath. I was to take the herb bath at midnight and at 3:00 in the morning every day for seven days.

Today I love to take a bath in the herbs because I believe they cured me. I was in a sad situation, but I am very grateful to my Uncle Joe for helping me. That's another example of witchcraft.

Chapter 16

Strange People

On these islands there were a few good people, just like every other place. There was a young man who was about 35 years old named Jonas. He was a very hard worker who loved his wife. He was a trustful husband. He and his wife had a beautiful relationship and they loved their kids very much. You didn't find that kind of love in a lot of people on the island. Then one day, a man named Cabrinho asked Jonas to help with some work that he needed done on his house. Jonas said, "I'm sorry, I cannot do it because I have other things to do for myself." Cabrinho got upset and decided to use Voodoo to kill him. Jonas became sick; he had a fever and pain all over his body. He couldn't explain just what he had. In seven days the man was pronounced dead and his young wife was left with three kids to raise. Cabrinho told her himself that he used witchcraft and he got away with it because no one did anything about it. It was not like today when a person might go to jail. At that time, especially in that remote part of the island, it was allowed.

There was very little law enforcement, especially if you were poor; you had no name and no credibility. When you didn't have money, you didn't have prestige, so people didn't believe you. That's how it was with me. I was nobody. I was nothing, so why should anyone listen to what I had to say? As for all the things that happened to me with Voodoo, I just endured them. I used to be a very innocent person. Whatever people did to me was okay. I couldn't talk, I couldn't cry, I couldn't laugh. Everything was okay. That was the attitude that I took to survive. If I were to say anything, I would have gotten a beating. So, I just took all that abuse and stuffed it deep inside of me.

Chapter 17

Witchcraft during San Felipe, 1967-68

I believe the black magic of witchcraft is from the people who are the witches themselves. This story happened on the other side of my island in 1967 to 1968. Far away from us was a family, who were known as witches—a mother and two brothers. They flew on Friday night. I used to have a friend named Jorge, who was around my age of 21when this happened. He was a hard worker and he was good looking. I was married, but he had a crush on me and I had a crush on him. Jorge worked in construction and he didn't get paid the week before the celebration for the saint we call San Felipe. The people celebrated that saint in his village on that part of the island. It was a beautiful way to celebrate with drums, music, dance, and a lot of food. A lot of young ladies and young guys would go to the celebration to have fun and check each other out. Jorge wanted to buy some nice clothes to wear to the celebration, but he was short on money.

Jorge borrowed money from the witch man called Pop. Pop had a store and his family had a good income. It was going to be two weeks before Jorge got paid from his job and then he was going to pay Pop back. Jorge bought himself some shorts, some pants, and some nice-looking shirts to wear to the celebration festival. Pop decided he didn't want to wait for two weeks to receive his money, so he decided to ask Jorge for his money back. Pop asked to meet him at work.

Jorge told him, "I don't have the money right now. I get paid next Friday; I'll give you your money then."

Pop said, "No, I want my money right now. If you don't pay me my money before Friday, you aren't going to make it to Friday." But Jorge took it as a joke. A lot of people said Pop was a witch, but Jorge did not want to believe it. A lot of people didn't believe in witches and Voodoo, no matter where they were from. The next day Jorge didn't make it to work because he was sick. His family didn't believe in witches either, even though they had seen all the Voodoo things that were done to other people. They were Catholic, they went to church, and their religion didn't let them believe in those kinds of things.

When I heard Jorge was sick, I went to visit him. When I got to his house, he was in bed. He was crying and screaming. He knew he was dying. He had a terrible fever and all kinds of ailments. Nobody knew what it was. While Jorge was dying, he started to talk but it wasn't his voice that we heard. It was Pop's voice. Pop's family was there at Jorge's house because Jorge was very good friends with Pop's niece and nephew and with everybody in the family.

Then Pop's voice was heard coming out of Jorge and he said, "I am so embarrassed, because I have a lot of family here who know me and know that I did this. I'm sorry, but I have to go." The house Jorge lived in was very close to the ocean, just a few yards away. When Jorge died, a black cat flew from inside the house straight to the ocean. Believe me, I was there.

My sister-in-law's mother was there also and she said, "Oh, Demon, you killed him! You are nothing but a son-of-a-bitch!" Then everybody started to cry and scream. About an hour later we all walked from Jorge's house past Pop's house on the way to church. There sat Pop in front of his house and he looked exactly like a cat. I can still see his face now. He was so tired. His eyes were sunken in and he looked sick.

My sister-in-law's mother shouted at him, "Look at your face. You should be ashamed of yourself. Why don't you get into somebody like me? You know, you can't get into me!"

Pop and his family got a lot of people sick and took a lot of people's lives. He tried to get into me also, to get rid of me, but I have a gift from God.

Those witchcraft spells could affect me only so much, but they didn't affect me all the way. I always got help. Thank God, thank you Jesus. Even if I didn't know where God was, I still would believe deeply. God is somewhere, God is everywhere, and God is good to me.

Chapter 18

Bina Becomes Frozen

Some of my friends and I walked to a part of the town that had a lot of ditches and hills. As we walked toward this area, I saw Pop in my mind's eye. Before I actually saw him, I knew he was coming. When we did see him, I stopped. As he passed by me, he wanted to say "Hi" and touch me, but I moved. I didn't let him get to me. After Pop passed, I froze and couldn't move at all. I couldn't move one step forward or one step backward.

No one in front of me looked back to see if I was close to them. Finally, someone started to talk to me. They called my name but they couldn't hear me answer. When they turned back to look at me, I was still in the same spot.

The oldest lady in the group said, "Wait a minute. That was Pop, the son of a bitch, ugly." She kept calling him all kinds of names as she made the sign of the cross. She walked back to me, made a cross and prayed and asked me to give her my hand. She kept making the cross and told me to touch the cross. She kept praying; I don't know what she prayed. I took a breath and started to move. I can never forget this.

I don't know if this man had a crush on me. Every time I went to this part of town, he always looked at me with that funny smile. But he was an old man and I was still in my twenties. When he came to the United States, I believe it was in the 1970s, he asked somebody about me. He wanted my phone number, but the person, thank God, didn't have it. Pop asked for my phone number from somebody else and this person called me to ask if he could give him my phone number.

I said, "Hell, no! I don't want to talk to that man, and I don't want him to be close to me. I don't want him to be in my house, I don't want to have nothing to do with him!" But you know God doesn't like ugly and God doesn't like us to do anything bad. This man's store fell apart slowly all the way to the ground. Pop had the saddest life to end with and I don't know how he died.

When my stepson's aunt had a son by Pop's brother, the nephew moved in with his grandmother who was the witch mother. The son was four or five years old and his father, his grandmother, and his Uncle Pop were teaching him how to fly on Friday nights. A month later, the boy came back home to spend the weekend with his mother. He told his mom about a beautiful party he went to.

His mom asked, "What party did you go to?"

He said, "We went to the party in the ocean."

His mom asked, "What ocean?"

He said, "There were a lot of people there. Mom, we flew, we didn't walk."

Poor thing! When his mom started to discover what was going on, she said, "No, I don't think you are going there anymore." But he started to fall in love with those fun things because he was a kid, of course. But his mom took him away from that family.

There was another young lady that was bewitched. She had a spell put on her by Pop's brother. She was beautiful with dark hair and dark skin. This man was crazy for her, but she never cared for him. She could not have any other man as long as this man was alive because he didn't let her. He would make her do embarrassing things. It didn't matter where she went, if he wanted her to be embarrassed, he controlled her. He made her take her clothes off in public. He made her scream, and she made ugly noises. A lot of people thought she was crazy, because most people didn't see the man do anything. She was the only one who saw him and knew what he was doing. Even if she told the people around her, they didn't believe her.

This man told her each time before it happened, "On such and such day, I am going to do something to you. If you go to this party you are going to regret it."

When she went, she did regret it because he made her do things out of her control. Those things happened for a long time while I was still in the islands. I didn't ever hear about what happened after that. Pop and his family were a bad bunch.

Chapter 19

BINA IN 1967

In 1967 and 1968, I continued to sleep on the floor. My mom would send me money and clothes. Then everybody liked me. My mother-in-law was nice to me, the girlfriend would not come by and I started to sleep in the bed again with my husband. It was because I had all these nice things coming to me from my mom. My husband started to hold my hand and tell me he loved me. After a while when they had gotten everything I had—all the money, all the clothes—I didn't mean anything to them anymore.

One morning while I was at home with my husband and his mother, we heard a knock at the door. A man said, "We are looking for Bina. She is under arrest."

Neither my husband nor mother-in-law asked why, they just gave me to them. I wondered if they were trying to set me up. The person who sent the police to come arrest me was high up in the police force and was my husband's cousin's husband. Even now I do not know why I was arrested.

I moved to the U.S. in 1969 but I came back to visit home in 1975. Upon my return, the first people I saw that I knew were my mother-in-law and the man who arrested me. When they saw me, I could see all the guilt they held on their faces. I said hello and they responded but they looked so guilty they couldn't even smile. We went our separate ways never to see each other again.

Chapter 20
Bina Has Twins, 1968

I went to stay at the Sossa's home and continued to spend my nights there. My husband and mother-in-law did not care that I slept there. For nearly a month I'd been sleeping over at Mrs. Sossa's, when I met a young man. He was Mr. Sossa's nephew; he was about 18 and I was 21. Even though I was a few years older than he was, I didn't look it, because I was so thin. His name was Antonio.

At first I didn't like him, but after a while I began to have a little crush on him and I knew he liked me. When he found out I was spending the nights at his uncle's house, Antonio said, "You know Bina, if you don't go home, you might as well go home with me. I live alone and I have a bed for you. You'll move in with me and you can sleep in my bed every night."

I got to know him better and as I fell in love with him, some people started saying that he and I should get together. I went home and packed up what clothes

I had left. I had given away nearly everything, and I moved in with Antonio. It was a big deal at the time. It was a big deal in my family because nobody knew what was going on with my husband. I believe up to this day, my sister and my brother didn't know I was sleeping on the floor. My uncles and my aunts didn't know. It was the time my husband and my mother-in-law beat me up.

A few months after moving in with Antonio, I started to show. I told him, "I think I am pregnant, but it cannot be yours because of the months."

He said, "It's okay, I will take care of the baby." Then one day we were talking about who loved who. He said, "Bina, I love you. You didn't love me, I made you love me."

I said, "What do you mean you made me love you?"

He told me he took a picture of me, a lock of my hair, and paid 400 dollars to a guy to put Voodoo on me so that I would fall in love with him. After that, I started to feel like I didn't love him as much anymore. I had stayed in contact with my husband because he still wanted to come to the United States.

After a few more months, I was ready to go into labor. It was November 28, 1968, when I was 22 years old that I had my baby girl. It was a very small, dark room. From across the street, a neighbor brought a light so we could see to cut the umbilical cord. Antonio brought some wood to make a fire and three ladies came to help me with my delivery. When my baby girl arrived, I still had a big stomach. One lady said she thought I had another baby in there. I stood there waiting for the placenta to come out, and I felt something move inside me. It was half an hour after the baby girl was born, that I bent my knees and another baby came out. It was a baby boy. Very few people had twins in those days.

My daughter was named Lina Alves, and she was white with blond hair and green eyes just like my husband's mother. A lot of people accused me of having a baby by a white man. What saved me was my baby boy, Lino Alves; he was very light-skinned but you could tell he would be dark skinned because his lips and nipples were dark. José Cana said they were not his babies, but my son looked exactly like my husband. He didn't want to have anything to do with the babies.

It was exciting to have twins because they were uncommon. Everyone seemed happy about them. Antonio had two sisters named Jacinta and Magna. I asked them to be godmothers for my babies. My twins were beautiful. There were a lot of people who came by to see them. About a month after they were born, this particular 50-year-old lady we called Mulata, passed by. I heard people say she was a witch, but I didn't pay much attention at the time when she came to the house. She always tied a scarf around her head over her left ear. It had been cut off because someone caught her doing Voodoo.

She said, "Bina, I came because I heard you had the most beautiful babies." Both babies were on the bed. She looked at them and said, "Ooh! Bina, these babies are too beautiful for you. You can't keep them. They don't belong to you."

I didn't say anything to her; I just looked at her. Because I had a very low opinion of myself, I didn't always know what to do.

She said, "I'm leaving, but I expect I'm gonna hear something about these babies not being here anymore."

I was so stupid. This woman put a spell on me and my babies. She cursed my babies and I didn't even realize what happened. She had never been to my house before and by the way she acted, I think she went there just to do this.

After she left it started to happen. It only took about three days. Whatever the babies ate they would vomit up. I breast-fed them and they threw up and had terrible diarrhea. Everything came out of them, poor things. I didn't have enough milk, so I mixed water with sugar and gave it to them. I didn't know what to do to take care of them or know how to make a medication for them. We didn't have a really good doctor; we only had a clinic. In the clinic, there was a nurse who helped sick people.

I called Antonio's sisters, the babies' godmothers. I wanted to take them to the clinic and they came to pick us up. The nurse did as much as she could.

We stopped at the church to see if the priest would bless Lina and Lino. As soon as we got in the church the babies' faces turned pink. One nun at the church told the girls to not let me see the babies because they might die before we got home.

I was so depressed because my babies were going to die. That night, I slept with my baby boy while breast-feeding. When I woke up and touched him, he was ice cold and stiff. I started screaming.

My godfather was a carpenter. Someone had told him that one of my kids had died so he sent me a message that he would make the coffin for my baby. I believed at the time that we had to find someone to bury the baby. No one would take off work and we would have to force someone to bury my son. I was sad but was glad I still had my baby girl. Three days after my son' funeral I was feeding my little girl and milk started coming out of her eyes, nose and ears. I held her up not knowing what to do. Her arm rolled back and she went limp. She died in my arms. I screamed and everyone came running but there was nothing anyone could do. My family would not talk to me at the time because of what was happening with my husband, and my sister, Zita, did not like Antonio because he was black.

It was the same time that one of my aunt's daughters died also. When my son died, I did not see anyone from my family. When they heard my daughter died, they decided to come see me. Sometimes I wonder if it was my fault my baby died; sometimes I blame myself. I keep asking myself if there was something I could have done about it.

My aunt asked me who was the last person to come by and I told her it was Mulata. My aunt asked me what Mulata had said, so I told her.

She said, "Why didn't you slap her and send her to hell? You let people take advantage of you!" She told me that Mulata was the one who killed the babies and that she was a witch. Later, other people told me the same thing.

Voodoo hurts and it kills. Believe me, Voodoo kills. I lost my babies and I was so unhappy. After almost one year together, Antonio and I broke up. 1968 was an awful year for me.

Chapter 21
ME AND PETER, 1970-71

Even after all of this, my husband still wanted me so he could come to the United States. We took a boat to go to Brava so I could say goodbye to my son who was living with his grandparents. From there we took a plane to Portugal. We waited in Portugal for three months for the paperwork to be completed. From there we took another plane to come into the United States.

My husband José Cana and I lived together for a few months here in the States with my mom in Roxbury, Massachusetts. We finally agreed to separate in the fall of 1970. In November my mom gave me a birthday party for my 24th birthday. There were people from our neighborhood at the party and I was flirting and having fun with everybody. I wore my light blue and white dress with ruffles; a style we called back in the islands "Three Marias" because the dress had three layers of ruffles. As I walked around the house, I noticed a young man who was around my age.

He wore a gray suit with a white shirt and black shoes. His hair was black and curly and he had a very nice complexion. His eyes looked like he could have some Asian blood mixed in, but when I met his mom, she was a tall, beautiful, white woman with light brown hair. I saw that he was checking me out, and I pretended not to notice. After most of the guests had left the party, he was still there. He then approached me and asked if I was the one who had this birthday party.

I said, "Yes," and we started talking. After some small talk, he left and came back for a friendly visit on Sunday. We got to know each other a little bit better and slowly he worked his way into my life. We decided to move in together and rented a house nearby.

His name was Peter. I knew I liked him very much, but because of past experiences, I didn't know how to tell if he loved me or if he just wanted to use me like most men. I was confused because I really never knew what love was. I never had anyone love me for who I was. Peter didn't know anything about my past and I really didn't want to tell him. We had a good thing going; we had a good relationship, or at least I thought we did. But then I found out that he was cheating on me.

I started to wonder when one weekend we went to a party in the neighborhood. At these parties, usually everybody dances with everybody else because it is a Creole custom. Peter had a drink or two and I saw him dancing with this very shapely young woman named Nana. When it came to a slow dance, I noticed that Peter was enjoying holding Nana in his arms. I felt like he was getting too close to her. I watched in disgust. Peter's friend must have seen that I was not too happy with what was going on, because he came over and asked me to dance to keep me busy.

Out on the dance floor I tried to get close to where Peter was dancing, but his friend kept moving me around. Then at the next slow dance I just couldn't take it anymore. I marched over to Peter and pushed him away from Nana and I slapped him good. I rushed out of the party to go home. He ran after me. I ran away from him in my high-heel shoes. I was so angry. When we got home, he explained that he didn't do anything on purpose to make me mad. That night we talked and worked things out so everything was okay.

We had discussed getting a bigger house, so I thought a move would be a good idea. We moved from Clarence Street to a house on Alban Street. Once in a while, we would have friends over for lunch or dinner and things seemed to be going well. But I found out that he was still seeing other girls. I worked days and he worked nights, so during the day he had some time to fool around.

One day one of the ladies in our neighborhood, someone who I thought was our friend, came to me and said, "Bina, I have been hearing people visiting Peter after you have gone to work. Sometimes Peter leaves home early and stops at my brother's house before going to work. And sometimes my niece, Nana, has come over to spend time with Peter in your house instead of going to school." She continued, "I listen to every step he takes when he comes home at night." She told me this, but I didn't realize what she really meant. Later I found out that she too was spending time with Peter.

One particular morning I got up with a funny feeling that something was going on in the house. I left home and headed for the bus stop where I usually caught the bus to go to work. When I got to there something was nagging at me to stay home from work that day. I turned around and went back home. It was about a quarter to seven when I put the key in the door and opened it. Guess who was there? It was a girl from the apartment house above us. She was sitting at the kitchen table with Peter. You should have seen their faces when they saw me.

The girl said, "Oh, I thought you went to work."

I said, "No, I changed my mind." Peter got up from the table with such a foolish smile and with a look of guilt all over his face.

The girl then uttered, "I just came down for some sugar."

I asked her, "Okay, where is your cup for the sugar?"

She mumbled, "I guess I didn't think about bringing a cup." I was so dumb that I just gave her some sugar and didn't realize what was going on.

I caught Peter one more time and this time it was with one of the high school girls. Actually, it was the one he finally married. I went to the neighbor's house because they had a phone. I asked them to call the police for me, because my English was still not very good.

When the police came to take Peter away, he said, "Bina, don't let me go. If you let me go, I will never come back. The woman that kicks me out only kicks me out once." I didn't want to listen to him anymore. I knew I had feelings for him, but I was so mad at him for fooling around on me that I didn't want him anymore. And this time, I was stubborn about it.

About a month later, I found out that I was pregnant. I was working at Plymouth Rubber Co. and I seemed to always be tired. I was sleeping a lot. One of my supervisors inquired, "Bina, you have a Bambino?"

I remarked, "No, it can't be!" But because I was so tired all the time, I went to the doctor. The doctor confirmed that I was about two months pregnant.

I called Peter and told him. He said, "I knew you were. I knew by the way your attitude changed." It was a strange thing, but I was faithful to Peter while I carried his child. After the baby was born, I stayed faithful; I saw no other man. Peter came to the Boston

City Hospital when my sister, Zita, called him to tell him I was going into delivery. In 1971, I had a very tough delivery, but I had a beautiful baby boy. We named him Francilino Mario Alves. Peter came to visit Francilino several times. After he was married, Peter even brought his wife to visit the baby a few times. But then we lost touch and I raised my son by myself and Peter had nothing else to do with Francilino.

After Peter, I started to get crazy again like I was in the islands. That was the reason, I do believe, that a lot of the older people back east looked at me like I was the same old Bina I used to be. But I was not. It was just my low self-esteem, and the only thing I knew was that people could take advantage of me. The best thing that happened to me in my whole life was to move from Massachusetts to live in California.

Chapter 22

MY GUARDIAN ANGEL

My guardian angel has protected me all my life. He protected me from getting killed so many times. I had come to the United States on May 14, 1969, to Boston, Massachusetts. In June, I got a job at a place called Tremont Street. I had to walk to work. It was about a 20-minute drive but I did not drive at that time. There were no houses around, just the street and fields with bamboo trees.

I saw a young black man with a big afro wearing a white shirt and black pants. I will never forget that day. He was walking toward me on the same side of the road. As soon as I saw him, something came over me, telling me to cross the road to avoid this man, but he crossed the road also. There was no one around and no houses; it was an empty, quiet place. When he came up to me, I couldn't understand him because I still didn't know any English. The only word I understood was "money". I had been warned from the people of my country about the black people in America and how they would steal all your money.

I gave him my purse with my passport and everything in it but he was still not satisfied. He crossed my arms against my chest. He held my hands with one hand while he pulled out a gun with his other hand and put the gun to my head. I believe he knew I did not speak English. I couldn't say anything to him. In the meantime, a car came from out of nowhere and the person stopped and honked his horn. When the man turned around and saw the car, he grabbed everything and jumped into what must have been a ditch with tall grass, because I could not see him anymore. Now in my heart, I felt kind of sorry for him. I thought he might die! I don't know why, but I was concerned about him and here he was trying to kill me!

I turned to walk back home. There were many businesses where I walked to Dudley Station. I felt safer there. I saw this car that belonged to a friend of the family. The car door was unlocked, so I opened the door and got inside. The owner of the car was in the store.

When Berto walked up to his car, he saw me there and said, "Bina?" I was sitting there crying. He said, "What's the matter, what are you doing in my car?"

I cried, "This black man jumped me, took my money, took my purse and put a gun to my throat. He was going to kill me!"

Berto looked at me and asked," How many of them?"

I said, "Just one."

He looked at me and said, "You are lucky. Last week I had five men jump me and they broke my arm." Berto drove me home to my mom's house where I was living. It was about 10:30 in the morning. My mom got really scared when she saw me.

She said, "What has happened to you?" This was the first time I felt my mom support me. She said, "Let's go there and pick up your check. You will not work there again. We will find you another place to work."

We went there that afternoon and picked up my money. It was a very close call and I know that it had to be my guardian angel that brought that man to that spot at that exact moment for him to honk his horn. Thank you, Jesus, for providing me with a guardian angel.

Chapter 23

WITCHCRAFT ON MOM, 1972

In 1972, my mother started to talk kind of funny and would say crazy things. The family didn't know what she was talking about. She acted really weird. One day, she was changing her clothes in her bedroom. I passed by her room and I saw her head turn. Her face turned from where the face was supposed to be to the back of her neck and she started to shake. She turned into a completely different person. She then became so sick she had to go to the hospital. When they put her in the car to take her to the hospital, she wanted to open the car door to get out because she didn't want to go.

It was so spooky how that witchcraft Voodoo stuff worked. There were so many different kinds of evil things that people did to each other. I didn't even know which one was which. I didn't know if it was witchcraft, black magic, white magic, bad eyes, or bad imagination. I didn't know but I'm telling you, whatever it was, I know it was not from God.

My mother was not totally cured, but she felt a little bit better with some medication that came from Lisbon, Portugal. When I wrote this book, my mom was still alive and she was still sick from the illness that made her act weird. But I saw it with my own eyes. I know it is hard to believe something like this, unless you're there to actually see it yourself. It was like that scene in the movie *The Exorcist* which I have never seen, but was explained to me. I saw how my mom acted weird, how she was aware of it, how she turned her face to the back of her neck. The back of her head was where her face was supposed to be. It was just so spooky how witchcraft could do that.

Chapter 24

JOHN-JOHN, 1972

In the summer of 1972, I met an African American man. His name was John, but I liked to call him John-John. He was a huge black man with big lips and a nice body. He had everything a woman needed in a man. But John-John had some problems—he was abusive and very jealous. While we were dating, I decided to buy a car even though I didn't drive. It was a nice Pontiac convertible—light yellow with a black top. I didn't drive my car, but John-John drove it. Yeah, he drove it with any woman he wanted, but me. He took them to the store, he took them to the movies, and anywhere he wanted to go. As for me, I had to take the bus wherever I needed to go—to work, to the store, any place I wanted to go. He figured out that I still couldn't speak English very well.

I had just come to the U.S. three years before, and John-John thought that I didn't have the right to go with him because I couldn't speak the language well. After that, I decided to break it off with him. My brother Adrian knew John-John was abusing me.

One day John-John pinned me against the wall. He put a big knife against my throat and he said, "Bina, I don't want to kill you but I have to." He was a very dark-skinned man but the color of his skin kept changing—flashing red, white and green. It was very scary to see this happen. Then, when he stuck the knife up to my throat, I was even more scared.

Right at that moment we both heard a knock three times on the other side of the wall. John-John asked me, "Do you expect anybody?"

I replied with a trembling voice, "No." It was strange because the knock came from the other bedroom, not from the door. He went to look in the room and nobody was there. We both went to the front door and looked and no one was there either.

This was my guardian angel protecting me again! I told John-John to give me the knife. He looked at me with his big eyes and gave it to me. He started apologizing and I told him he needed to get help. He started to cry and said he would not hurt me anymore. He hugged me, kissed me, and I told him I forgave him.

About a month later I needed to go to the store for something, so I called John-John. I asked him to come home and we got into it again over the phone. He was really upset with me because I had called him. He was busy. When he got home, he started arguing with me. He threw me on the bed, slapped me, and then started choking me with both hands around my throat. I could not breathe and felt like I was losing consciousness.

Then something happened. I started to feel a strength come over me. I pulled both my legs up and pushed him in the stomach, sending him flying across the room. He looked surprised because I only weighed about 99 pounds. He got up and rushed back  to me and I started scratching and hitting him—any way I could fight back. I scratched him on the face and he started bleeding. Again John-John threw me on the bed and started choking me when we heard a knock at the door. This time, somebody knocked on the front door. We answered the door and it was a life insurance man who came to collect money. That was the last time we had a fight, because I kicked him completely out of the house.

He knew where I worked and he knew what time I came home. I lived on the second floor of an apartment complex that had a basement. He and one of his friends broke into the basement to get inside. They broke into my apartment and took my money, my TV, and some gold I had brought from my country. He took everything he knew was of value to me. I found out it was him because some people on the first floor saw him, but were afraid to call the police.

When I got home, I found my back door broken into and I started to check around my apartment. I noticed all my stuff was gone. I think he did it out of revenge for my kicking him out of my life. That same day, I called my brother, Adrian, to let him know what was going on. He drove right over and parked his car in front of the apartment. John-John and his friend drove by to see if I was home. I guess he wanted to see how I would react when I found my apartment broken into. When he saw Adrian's car, he and his friend flattened all four tires. My brother and I were watching through my window. He knew we were watching because he looked up and saw us. Adrian and I were both scared. My brother was only 17 years old and I did not want him to go down there. We called the police, but by the time they got there, John-John and his friend had gone. My brother thought a lot of John-John because he was like a brother to him. Also, Adrian was dating John-John's niece, Cynthia, and it was hard on them to know we had broken up.

A few weeks later, while Adrian was driving his red convertible with a friend, he was stopped at a traffic light. John-John pulled up next to him and pointed a gun at my brother's head.   John-John said, "I want your sister back. If I don't have her, I am going to kill you because I know she is not with me because of you."

Maybe a week later, I went to a store called Dave's on the corner by mother's house. It was the summer time and I was wearing white hot pants with a nice flowery top. I felt somebody behind me, watching me. When I turned around, it was John-John. He had tears in his eyes. I glared at him and walked away. I said to myself, *I don't want to go back to him; I just want him to leave me alone.* He tried to talk to me, but I would not answer him; I kept walking.

Chapter 25
LUCIANO, 1973

John-John left me alone for about three months, but he didn't like to see me with anybody else. In his mind, he thought we would get back together again. He could not stand the thought of my having another boyfriend. John-John got very angry and jealous when he saw me with my new boyfriend. Luciano was from my country. He was very respectful and treated me like a lady. Luciano stayed with me in my house every night. I knew his family and his sister, Mariazinha. She was a very good friend to me.

Mariazinha, her five children, and her mother lived together, because her mother and father were separated. Luciano's father lived on the same street as John-John. One night Luciano and I were asleep in bed. While he slept, his body kept shaking like he was having a seizure. I placed my hand on his forehead to see if he had a fever and asked him if he was okay. He said, yes, but he had a headache and his body kept shaking. I got up to get him some medicine and heard someone knock on the door. It was about 2:30 in the morning. When I went to the door and asked who was there, it was Luciano's brother-in-law's nephew. I asked him what he wanted with Luciano at that time of night. He said he was there to take him home, that something was wrong. I asked him what it was and he said that Mariazinha had a fight with her husband and Luciano needed to come home.

When I opened the door and I saw his face, I knew there was something more to it. His face was so sad. He didn't want to tell me what was going on. I went to my bedroom and told Luciano that someone was here to pick him up and take him home. It was like he knew something was wrong because he was already up and dressed.

He said, "Yes, I need to go home." I didn't sleep the rest of the night. I called over to Mariazinha's house but the phone was always busy.

I got up at about 7:00 the next morning. My mother lived across the street from my house and she opened the window and called to me. She said, "Bina, Mariazinha is dead.

I said, "What are you talking about?"

She said, "Mariazinha is dead and her five children; her mother and the other lady who lived there are dead too."

This was very heartbreaking news to me. Mariazinha was a wonderful person and I felt the loss of a good friend. It was also a tragedy in the community that day, because their home caught on fire and they all died in the fire. There were three other children who lived there on the second floor who survived, but were badly burned. They were left to grow up with scars on their faces and all the pain of the loss of their family.

A few days later, somebody wrote a note on a grocery store paper bag. The note read: ***Bina paid me to do this to this family***. Someone put this note in the mailbox of Luciano's father. I knew something was not right the next day when I went to visit Luciano's family. Mariazinha's husband looked very strange. He looked guilty. I didn't think anything of it at the time, because I had not heard anything. I went to the father; he shook my hand and he hugged me and we both cried. He knew I loved Mariazinha and her mother very much. They had welcomed me into their family with love.

When I shook the hand of Luciano's brother-in-law, I felt like something was not right. I sat down and noticed that people were talking and looking at me. They were whispering to each other and made me feel like I had done something wrong. I went to the kitchen and asked Luciano's father if I could make some coffee.

He said, "Yes, go make some coffee."

Luciano went to the kitchen with me and said, "Bina, you need a lawyer."

Innocently I asked, "Why?" I didn't know what he was talking about.

He said, "Because you wrote a letter to my father saying you paid someone to start the fire to kill all the family." I looked at him thinking he was kidding, and asked him if he was. He was very serious when he said, "No, I would not kid about something like that. I know you did not do it."

His father came into the kitchen and said, "Maria Bina, I know you would not do something like that. I know what kind of heart you have. We know you." He continued, "If they put you in jail, we will get you out because we know you would not do something like that."

I stopped making the coffee; I couldn't believe what was happening, so I returned to my mother's house. By the time I got there, my mom had already heard the news and was crying. I went to a bedroom in the house to be alone. Lilly, a lady friend from my country came to my mom's house. Lilly had helped us when we arrived in the U.S. because she spoke English well and she translated for us. She helped us with getting set up here and with all the paperwork.

She asked my mom, "Where is Bina?"

My mom told her, "She is in the bedroom."

Lilly came to me and said, "I'm not going to let you go to jail because I know you did not do this." I knew some people supported me, but others I did not know how they felt.

When it was time for the funeral, I went. Mariazinha's husband did not receive me right. When I shook his hand, it was like he would not accept me there like I had done something wrong. But he knew all along I didn't do it. There at the house was a detective who was a friend of the family. I talked to him and he said that the note I supposedly wrote to the family was at the police station.

I went home and called the police station. I talked to one of the policemen and he sent two officers to my home. I told him I wanted to see the note. They did not handcuff me, but escorted me to the car. One policeman said to the other, "I don't think it was her."

They took me to the police station and before they let me see the note, they had me write the same sentence to see if my handwriting was like that on the note. But my note did not match. I could hardly speak English and did not know how to spell the words. The police said I could go home. When they dropped me off at my house I was so upset. My friend Mariazinha had died. All her children had died and her mother. I cried aloud.

The lady who lived a floor below me, called and said, "Maria, any problem you have, talk to my husband, because he is a policeman and he can help you out." She was from Puerto Rico.

I was too embarrassed to call her husband or to talk to her about what was going on. I kneeled down and prayed to Our Lady of Fatima and asker her,

"May the person who wrote that note and pretended to be me not walk for the rest of his life, and that he not use his hand to write for the rest of his life." It could have been anyone. I didn't know who it was and, at that time, I didn't care.

Three days later, I heard that John-John had a stroke while playing cards with his friends. I never went to the hospital to see him and three years later he died. It was like my prayer had come true. I always thought John-John had a part in the fire because of his anger toward Luciano and me. I didn't know for sure if it was John-John who did it by himself, because he was a friend to Luciano's brother -in-law. For a long time people, even my good friends, thought I had done some Voodoo on John-John, causing his stroke. He had caused me a lot of hurt and pain. He was not a good man.

I was not proud of what happened, but I felt relieved because now John-John would leave me alone. I asked God to forgive me, because I had prayed for something to happen to the person who had written that note against me. I didn't ask for it to be John-John or anyone specific. I thank you Jesus, for watching over me and I know God don't like ugly. There were a lot of ugly things that John-John did to hurt me.

After the funeral, Mariazinha's husband came to my house asking me to date him. He had just buried five children, his wife and his mother-in-law. A couple of days later, he came to me and said, "Bina, with the kind of money I am going to receive from the insurance, we are going to be rich." To go off about the insurance money was not right.

I told him, "No! No! I couldn't do that." I was so upset with him because Mariazinha was my very good friend, and at that time, I was still Luciano's girlfriend; and secondly, he just buried his family. I had always liked the man very much and he was very nice to me. Mariazinha used to call me every day. The day of the fire I called her and she said she was very tired because she had been cleaning the house all day.

Everyone thought it was the husband who started the fire. He had called the fire department but had waited until the fire was too far along before he made the call. The last time I saw Luciano as a boyfriend was that night of the fire in 1973. About two weeks after the tragedy, Luciano met a girl from our country and they started to date. When I found out he was dating someone else, I left him alone. They later married and I never saw him again.

Chapter 26
CHICAGO MAN, 1976

I had been working for several years and I saved up enough money to move back to the islands in 1975. The first face that I saw when I got there was the man who had raped me from the time I was eight to nineteen years old. He was so embarrassed. He knew what I thought of him just by the way I looked at him. He turned his face, then he turned his back and he didn't talk to me at all. He didn't even stay in the same place where I was staying. He saw the look I gave him. He knew I was serious.

I was raped again when I came back to the U.S. in 1976. This time it was by a man who was my best friend's boyfriend. He was from Puerto Rico. A bunch of us would often get together and go to the racetrack. One time, when I went by myself, he was there but I didn't see him. He must have been watching me. As I was getting ready to leave, he showed up out of nowhere and asked for a ride. I gave him a ride in my car and while we were on the freeway, he told me to pull over. I asked him why, and the next thing I knew, he pushed a gun to my face. I pulled over close to the end of the freeway and he raped me. That was the last time I saw him. I never saw him around my best friend again either.

In 1976, I went with a young man from Chicago, Illinois. I was in my late twenties. It was not a sexual thing, but more of the way he treated me with romance, flowers, candy, and jewelry; it was just the little things, the attention that he gave me that made me feel so special. I had never had that kind of gentle attention given to me in all my life.

His name was James, but I called him my Chicago Man because he traveled from Chicago to Boston. Whenever James came to Boston, he made time to see me. When he got to Boston, he rented a very nice car to go visit me in Brockton. He was a vice president for a life insurance company. He was a good catch for any woman, but I just didn't know how to play my cards right. I treated him like all the other guys, but I should have known the difference because he treated me very special. He was the first man ever to walk shoulder to shoulder with me. He held my hand whenever we walked together. I really liked that.

James bought me presents like a little golden necklace and a butterfly pin. He took me out to a restaurant, a really nice place, where we talked, laughed, danced, and kissed. We left the restaurant and came back to a very, very expensive hotel. He had one hotel room for business, but he didn't take me there. He had rented a room with room service—with everything I needed. He treated me like a queen. With all that I had been through, I can never forget about how he treated me and I can never forget about him.

I remember the first night we went to the hotel. I went into the bathroom and I left the door open. There was a big mirror on the wall and while he was stretched out in bed, he saw me in my sexy baby blue lingerie. He watched me put lotion on my beautiful legs. He watched me dab some perfume on my body as I made myself smell good for him. When I turned around, I looked at him and he looked at me. He made a gesture with his face like he wanted to eat me up, and he made a soft "umm" sound. It was beautiful. He had watched everything I did and I didn't realize it. I had kind of put on a little show for him without knowing it.

I remember that special night so fondly and I'm sure he remembers it also. Chicago Man was very special to me There was one particular day I remember we went out and I wore white pants and white underwear with little flowers on them. He told me, "Sweetheart, you don't look right with those pants. Go change your panties. See, if you have black panties you can wear under those white pants."

I went inside and changed into black panties. Because I have dark skin, using the dark panties made wearing the white pants look really nice. I appreciated his concern and his input on how I looked. I was so pleased that he gave me that idea. Now from time to time, whenever I wear white pants or something light, or kind of see-through, I wear black underwear. And each time I do that, I remember my Chicago Man.

We continued to keep in touch and we stayed close friends. Anytime I called him, he returned my phone calls. He always made time to talk to me. I do believe I was special to him. We had a good connection. I have always kept in the back of my mind.

A few years later I came to California and I met my husband. I called James and told him I got married. Years later we talked again, and in the conversation he told me, "You're the one who went to California to get married. I didn't get married yet; you got married on me."

When I spoke to him late in 1986, he told me he had gotten married. It was something like a setup. He didn't want to have any more kids, but the lady became pregnant with his child. He and this lady believed in the same religion and so he had to marry her. I still believe that it was not for love. He did love his children, especially his first son.

We still keep in touch as friends. Why do I still keep in touch with this man? Because really, he was the first man who held my hand and walked with me. I liked this man; yeah, this Chicago Man.

Chapter 27

KIDNAPPED, 1977

Late in 1977, most of my friends were white. At that time there were a lot of prejudices going on that I didn't know about. I met Billy, a guy who was Italian and Irish. We met at the racetrack and started to date. He lived in Revere and I lived in Dorchester, Massachusetts. He would spend the night sometimes at my place. We had a good time. We would go to restaurants and nightclubs. At that time, I didn't know anything about drugs or the Mafia.

One day I met him at the racetrack and we went to the snack bar to have something to eat and we bet on a few races. I didn't win anything and I didn't think Billy won because he didn't tell me anything. We left the track and headed to my car in the parking lot.

There were two white guys walking behind us. They called, "Bill!" By their voices, I could tell they were Italian.

I turned around and looked at them. One had a gray jacket and black pants. I didn't notice how the other one was dressed. I didn't know the two guys, but I think Billy knew them because he said, "Let's keep walking to the car."

As soon as I turned back around, the man with the gray jacket came up to us and grabbed Billy by the arm and put a gun to his side. He said, "Okay, Billy, you and your girlfriend come with us."

We went with the two men and they put us in the back seat of their car. The car was light blue, maybe a Ford or a Toyota. After that, all I can remember was when we left the parking lot looking down on the racetrack.

The next thing I can remember was waking up and seeing a high mound with a deep ditch. I didn't know if they had drugged me, or what happened. I think I had been left there to die. I felt like I was in a very deep fog, like I was in the air. I saw myself like an angel; I was all in white, everything was white, even the ground. I saw a guardian angel also in white, flying in the air. I didn't know if it was me who had turned into a guardian angel, or if it was my guardian angel.

I then started to wake up more and when I realized I was walking. I was on the road headed into Woodland. I passed by the restaurant that we used to go to all the time. When I woke up, I didn't have my purse, but I still had the same clothes. I was able

to make my way to the train station. I
didn't know exactly how I got there; I didn't know what had happened to my car, I had no money, and I had no ticket. But I do believe my guardian angel was with me because I got on the train from Revere to Dudley Station in Roxbury. I got off of the train, onto a bus on Douglas Street. I walked home because it was not too far from my house. I didn't have a key, but somehow I opened the front door. When I got into my house, I went straight to bed.

All night I tossed and turned as I thought about what had happened to me. I knew that I went to the racetrack, I left the track with Billy and those two guys, and when I woke up in the air, I was all in white and I had wings. It had to be my guardian angel, because I had no power to be there up in the air myself. The next morning, I woke up and I took a shower. I got dressed and started to walk over to my mom's house. The kids were staying at my mom's. My mother had gotten up early that morning and was already in the street looking for me.

She saw me, put both her hands on her head and said, "I was so worried! Where have you been for three days?"

It was only at that time that I realized that I had been gone that long. I didn't tell my mother anything because she wouldn't believe me anyway. I didn't know what had happened to Billy. I never heard from him again. I knew I had nobody with me when I came to. I started to remember more of what happened.

I was a good friend with three sisters—they were triplets. They had been looking for me, because we went out almost every weekend. I was older, so I was the one who drove.

When one of them, Lizette, who was really close to me saw me she said, "I went to your house, I called you, you never answered." I said that I had been out. She asked me, "Who was this man who took you away for three days?"

I said, "Somebody kidnapped me and Billy."

She said, "Yeah, right!"

I told her I didn't know about what happened to Billy, but I tried to explain to her about what had happened to me. She believed a lot of what I said. I don't think she believed the part about how I had died and came back again. I had even forgotten that I told her anything until 1999 when we spoke about my being kidnapped. She told me she that remembered that. I still wonder to this day what happened to Billy.

I thank God every day when I get up and before I go to bed at night. I thank Jesus; I thank my guardian angel for being with me, because I know I have a very strong angel watching over me. I know, in my heart, I am not a bad person. I do so many things for people to help them; I feel their pain and emotions and I get close to them. My heart is there for everyone. Even with the hard life I had in the past, I do not harbor anger. I did so much good for others I didn't understand why those bad things happened to me. I do know God helped me, watched over me, took care of me, and brought me to my house. It was only God who could do this by giving me a guardian angel.

Chapter 28

PHIL FROM GUINEA, 1978

I met another man when I moved late in 1978 from Roxbury to Brockton, Massachusetts. This man spoke Creole and Portuguese—the same two languages that I spoke. His name was Phil, and he was another nightmare, another abuser. I don't know how in the world I kept getting involved with this kind of man. I didn't like him much. Phil didn't have a car either; he always drove mine.

I met Phil through my roommate. There was a club called West Gate Lounge in Brockton. We used to go there to have fun. There was something about him I didn't particularly care for but he kept talking to me and I decided to give him a chance. One time when we went to the club, he wanted to leave. I didn't want to go yet because we had just gotten there. He took me by the arm and with the other hand he punched me in the side as we walked to the door. He was clever. He always had a smile on his face so no one knew what was going on. He could stop and talk to someone with that smile and be punching me at the same time. All the women thought he was so special. He was the nephew of a President in Africa. He thought that every woman he liked he should get. Phil was the kind of man who had to have his way, one way or another.

One time we took a trip to Orlando, Florida. We spent the night at a motel that had a restaurant. I was not happy and it showed on my face. I was young and very sexy looking then, at least that was what I was often told. But this night my face showed that I was not happy. There were three truck drivers staring at me, and they could tell something wasn't right. I looked back at them. Phil grabbed me by the arm and asked me why the men were looking at me. I said I didn't know. He said you must know them from somewhere, but I didn't. He was going to go ask them why they were looking at me like that. He went over to them, but they didn't understand because he spoke in Creole. So, Phil wanted me to go over there and ask them why they were staring. I told Phil that I would translate for him, that if I went over there, I would ask them to beat him up.

That night, we went out to a nightclub in Orlando. I was not happy but it was a nice place. There were a lot of people and the music was good. Phil was wearing his dark sunglasses, even though it was night. Some guy made fun of him. He asked Phil how he could see with sunglasses in the nighttime. Phil took the glasses off and asked me why I didn't tell him he wasn't supposed to wear them at night. I said I didn't know. I hadn't even looked at his face because I was so unhappy.

I wanted him out of my life. One day he gave me a letter to mail for him. I put a stamp on it, but something told me to take the letter back. I told the postman I forgot to put something in the envelope. He gave me the letter. When I opened it, I found my picture, a piece of my clothing, and some of my hair. I went to a pay phone and called Eva, one of my girlfriends. Eva had a good education in my country and I asked her to meet me at the back door of my house. We met and went to the park.

Phil had written a letter to his aunt in Africa. He told his aunt in the letter that he wanted to do Voodoo to me to make me love him. He also wanted to do Voodoo on a white girl who was a millionaire. He wanted her family to like him, but he was black. If I had known about this other woman, I would have left him earlier. After we read the letter, I burned it with the money, the picture, and the piece of clothing. When I came home, he asked me if I had mailed the letter. I lied. For months he waited for a letter from his aunt but it never came. Meanwhile, I tried to get him out of my home.

My roommate, who shared my apartment, eventually moved out because she could not take what was going on there. She knew what was happening but I never talked about it with her; I was embarrassed and ashamed. One day, I saw Phil's former roommate at my children's godmother's house. I tried to tell him what was going on with Phil and me and that Phil had tried to kill me several times.

He responded, "If Phil wanted to kill you, he would have killed you a long time ago." That was his answer. I went to my car and cried. I felt so alone. It hurt my feelings that he wouldn't listen to me. It was the first time I had tried to talk to someone about what had happened to me and he didn't seem to care.

I worked nights and Phil worked during the day. I could not be more than five minutes late from work, or Phil would accuse me of being with another man. Every night when I was at work, Phil would have all his friends over for a party. They would always clean up and leave before I got home, but I could tell people had been there. I could tell someone had cooked, because the next day most of the food was gone. I noticed that two dozen eggs were gone. One day, a woman I worked with asked me if I knew what was going on while I was at work. She told me that besides the partying with his friends, Phil would also have his girlfriend over.

When I returned home after work, I could smell the scent of burnt candles. I found the candles, opened the window, and threw them out into the street. Sometimes the police came looking for

133

Phil, but they couldn't find him. Phil would always disappear.

One time, he picked me up from work and I asked him to take me to the police station. He asked why, and I said I had a ticket to pay. When we got to the police station, I told the police he is the one who was beating me up and I wanted him out of my house.

Phil put his hands on his head and started running in circles saying, "No, Maria, please don't do this to me! I can't leave you!" I felt sorry for him so I didn't press charges. When we got home, we went to bed but we couldn't sleep. We got into another argument.

Sometimes at 3:00 or 3:30 in the morning, he would drive my car and take me out to the park that had a big lake. At that hour of the morning, there wouldn't be anyone around. He would ask me if I was seeing someone else. He'd beat me up in the car. I remember one time it was a full moon and I could see everything clearly. I could see the clouds, the lake, and the big rocks. He took me there three different times in the middle of the night. Once when he told me to go with him, I put on my house robe, went to the kitchen, got a large knife and hid it in my sleeve. I told him I was not seeing another man. He got out of the car, picked up a big rock, and threw it into the windshield where I was sitting. I managed to get out of the car and saw how smashed the windshield was. I started to run and scream but no one could hear me. He chased after me; he caught me and took me back home.

I talked to the friend who introduced us and told him to get Phil out of my house. I showed him my black eye. I could tell Phil's friend felt bad. When I told Phil to leave, he said that he would.

He said, "I know this is not going to work." When I got home from work the next morning, I thought Phil had left. Instead, he took the suitcase that I let him borrow, and put it away. He said, "I'm not going to leave. Your sex is too good to let you be with another man." Phil said he was going to kill us both. I told him if he was going to do that, he should kill himself first, and then me last. In those days, I was so desperate that I even talked to someone who I knew was in the Mafia. I wanted him killed.

This Mafia guy asked, "What if I just cut off one arm, one leg, cut out one eye and cut off his manhood?" After thinking about it, I thought it would be better to just kill him. But I never followed through, I just talked about it. But I wasn't the only one who wanted him dead. The husband of another woman he had been seeing also wanted him killed.

Finally, Phil moved out and I thought I was going to get some rest, but he wouldn't leave me alone. He broke windows, doors, and followed me everywhere I went. I took him back again, because he promised he would never do anything again to hurt me. I thought maybe this time it was going to work out. What a fool I was again. I was still working nights. All evening I felt as though something was wrong. In my mind's eye, I kept seeing a woman lying down in my bed. While I was at work that night, about two hours into shift, I told my supervisor I did not feel well and asked if I could go home.

When I got home with all those feelings wrapped up inside of me, I should have been suspicious. I should have been smart enough not to park my car in my driveway. I recognized the car that was already there. When I got out of my car, I heard someone run to the front door. My eight-year old son, Junior, was there but he did not wake up. My son Manny was about 14 and he didn't wake up either. I don't know what Phil did to make them sleep so soundly. Our front door had a chain and I managed to break the chain and I forced my way into the house.

My bed was messed up, but there was no one there. This other woman, I guess in a way, was leaving me hints of what was going on. After sex with Phil, she washed herself off with a washcloth and left it on my bathroom counter; she left her cigarette butts also. I put all Phil's stuff in a box outside the door. When he came to the house, he broke a window to get in; he got a knife and gave it to me to kill him. I was so mad, I almost did.

He said, "I deserve to be dead, kill me! I don't deserve to be alive."

I told him, "I don't want to kill you. The best thing for you is to get out of here."

He pleaded, "I don't have any place to go, can I stay here?" The next day I called the police, but again they could not find him. He did move out, but kept following me everywhere I went.

One time Phil and I were on the way to a club and we stopped to get gas. There was a man following us. Phil walked up to the car and acted like he was going to shake hands, but instead, he punched him and hit him in the face with his head, smiling the whole time. He turned to me and started to hit me with his head. Other people there called the police. The next day, I called immigration because Phil did not have the proper legal papers to stay here. Finally, when immigration picked him up, they said there wasn't enough evidence to prove that he did what I said he did. Immigration said that he hadn't committed any crime, so they let him loose. They said he had some paper that let him stay in the country.

Around the same time, someone told me about a place called *Women Helping Women*. When I went there, they helped me find a shelter. But the day before I left home to move to the shelter, it rained heavily with lightning and thunder. I heard the window break. I had to replace a window almost every week. I saw his face, and I started to scream and so did my kids. We screamed loud. I had a neighbor who lived in the back of the house.

She opened the door, went out in the rain and yelled, "Send the Devil to Hell!" "Send the Devil to

Hell!" "Send the Devil to Hell!" three times. Phil turned around and left. I was so scared for the boys and me.

A lady I worked with told me that if I ever needed a place to go that I was welcome at her home. I took the kids to her house and I rang the bell. When she opened the door, I started to cry.   She asked, "Is it Phil again?"

I said, "Yes!" She changed my kids into some dry clothes and made them warm. She gave me some hot tea to make me warm also. I didn't go to work that night.

The next morning, I called *Women Helping Women*, and they helped me get into the shelter where I stayed a little over two weeks. They arranged for my employer to provide a security guard to walk with me from the factory to my car. I then drove directly to the shelter. Phil found out where the shelter was and he followed me. This time, the shelter called immigration on him. Immigration kept Phil for two months in Boston. Then the people from immigration called me because Phil had told them I was his wife. I told them I was not married to him, but they would not believe me. Phil's family bailed him out and when he saw my sister, he told her that he was going to find me.

Last I heard he had moved to Florida, but I didn't care. I don't know what ever happened to Phil and I really hope I never see him again. The people from the *Women Helping Women* organization helped me get to California. I was only to be in California for three weeks, but I didn't go back for six years because I met Leon.

Chapter 29

MET MY HUSBAND LEON, 1980

It was March of 1980 in Sacramento, California, that I met my husband, Leon Durham, and I was very happy. He was the sweetest man you could ever meet. It was the first time I fell in love in my life and I was 36 years old. I was 36 before I really had a man of my own besides my Chicago Man. My brother, Adrian, once told me, "If you leave this man, I will never talk to you for the rest of your life."

I married a black man but he was very gentle. I had a very serious problem with sexual things. When I met him, it took a long time for me to let him touch me. I always remember having the feeling of what happened to me in the past with black men.

CALIFORNIA

I first came to visit California with my youngest son and a friend, a nice man named Chris. We drove there from Massachusetts.

The first man I met in California became my husband. I didn't try at all to fall for this man. We met at a party and he gave me his phone number. For three months I kept the phone number, but I didn't call him. He sent a message through friends a couple of times to give him a call. One day I picked up the phone and called him. We made a date for breakfast and that was it. That was all it took.

The man is dead today, and no matter where he is, I still love him. He treated me like a lady when I met him. Let's just say that he was very special to me.

***

My friend had sent me a book. I've read a lot and watched a lot of shows. When I saw the commercial for *The Color Purple* in 1985, I knew that I had to go watch this movie. It was my first time going to the movies. I was almost 40 years old. The same things that happened to the girl in movie happened to me. I left there crying because the movie reminded me of myself so much.

The way Oprah acted in the movie was very similar to how my sister acted when my first husband beat me. My sister, Zita, was about 13 years old and she was strong and spirited.

She chased after my husband with a stick and she cried out, "I'm going to kill you, son-of-a-bitch! Leave my sister alone!"

It's sad, but my husband then looked at her and declared, "I gave it to your sister and I'm gonna give it to you too!"

Then, my sister and I, we both started to cry. When I was pregnant with my first child, they wanted to kill my baby. I spoke to the young lady who was supposed to kill my child. I told her that I didn't want to kill my baby. She said she was going to pretend that she was doing something to the child so they wouldn't beat her up. She said that she wouldn't kill my baby. Yes, I kept my baby. He is tall and very handsome and strong.

Chapter 30

SUSPICION ABOUT LEON, 1987

Late in 1987, my husband Leon had a car accident. He was disabled for three months and could not work. I was the one who worked and paid for everything, like I should, because I was his wife. One day he came home from court and I asked him how everything was going with his court case. He never told me anything, but said it was going okay.

I had a friend who was a lawyer. I couldn't find out anything from my husband. Six months had gone by and he was back to work and I started getting suspicious. I asked my friend what I could do to find out what was going on with my husband's case.

He asked, "What do you mean?" I told him my suspicions. When he checked into it, he found that there was nothing going on in court. So, I just let it go.

Sometime later, between 1988 and 1989, my oldest son, Manny came to me and said, "Mom, look! He gave me $100. He told me not to tell you, but he got his settlement."

To keep my son safe, I didn't let my husband know I knew anything. Our friends knew he had gotten the settlement, but he never told me and I was his wife. It turns out he had settled out of court. Leon had put all the money in his kids' names and his mother's name. My husband never told me how much money he got. But it must have been a lot.

My husband took a vacation every year to Cleveland, Ohio to see his mother. During our first five-to-six years, I never went on vacation with him. One particular year, about 1987, after the accident, it was just my son and me at home alone. Junior was only 13. He was sleeping in his bedroom. It was about 2:30 in the morning and I was in a deep sleep. I was dreaming and I saw this man walk behind my house. In my dream, I could see everything about this man. I could describe him perfectly. I knew who this person was in my dream, but when I woke up, I couldn't see him. He had light skin and a beard. He was walking in my driveway, behind and around the house to my bedroom. This man had stopped to pee.

I heard a voice saying, "Maria, wake up, somebody is going to kill you." This voice said this over and over again. I tried to wake up, but kept telling myself I was having a dream, so I fell back to sleep. I kept hearing the voice say, "Maria wake up, somebody is going to kill you." Even though I was not awake, I could hear a noise. I thought it was the icemaker dropping ice, but the noise didn't stop. The voice told me again, "Maria, somebody is going to kill you. Get up!"

That time I woke up; I sat up and put my feet on the floor. I kept hearing the noise and told myself the icemaker couldn't be making that noise. I went into the hallway from my bedroom and turned on the light. As soon as I turned on the light, I heard someone jump and then run.

I went into my son's room and said, "Junior, wake up! Someone has broken into the house!" I went to the back door and found the door lock broken. The only thing that saved me, besides my guardian angel and God, was the chain. The noise I had heard was the man trying to break the chain. For some reason, that night before I went to bed, I had moved the loveseat to block the front or back door. I don't know why I did that, but when I got to the door, the chair was pushed out as far as the chain would allow the door to be opened.

I was scared, so I called Arthur, a neighbor who was one of our friends. Arthur was a very nice man. Once Leon and I got into an argument and Arthur told him, "If you want to divorce her, go ahead, and I will marry her tomorrow. You don't know what a good wife you have."

I called Arthur and asked him to please call the police for me because somebody tried to break in. So, Arthur called the police. When the police came, they looked and saw the broken door lock.

After they left, Arthur called my husband in Cleveland. He told him, "I'm sorry to call you at this time, but I wanted to let you know that someone tried to break into your house. Maria called me to help her with the police."

My husband inquired, "What the hell are you doing at my house at 4:00 in the morning with my wife?"

I knew who this person was in my dream, but when I was awake, I didn't know him. A friend of the family looked exactly like the man I dreamed of, who had broken into our home. When my husband came home, he was not concerned about the break-in. We had nothing anyone would want. We had no jewelry or anything anyone would want to steal. The thing that was interesting was that my husband did not want to fix the door.

The next year my husband went on vacation and the door was still not fixed. All year round, all we had was the chain. After my husband left for vacation, my son and I would not sleep in the house alone. We stayed with friends. I was afraid to sleep at home with the broken door lock.

One day Leon's mother called and said, "Where have you been? My son has been worried about you."

"Well, if your son cannot find me, it's because I do not want to sleep here with the broken door lock. Have you ever seen me or met me, after these seven years of marriage?" I questioned her.

She said, "No!"

I said, "Don't you think that at least once my husband could have taken me with him to meet you?"

After he came home, he said, "Next year, we will go on vacation together to my mom's." The following year, when the month came to go see his mom, I refused to go because he didn't really want to take me; it was more for his mom wanting to see me, and that just didn't feel right to me.

I had a Mexican friend named Tanya—a very smart young lady. She would come to the house when my husband was not there. She saw things that were not right, but I could not pick them out. I still could not speak much English. One time she was at our house and she found stock certificates on the kitchen table. They had been there for a couple of weeks. I didn't know what they were but Tanya did. She told me that they were stocks for Proctor and Gamble, the company where my husband had worked for 30 years. Tanya started looking in the drawers where he kept his papers and she found a life insurance policy on me for $500,000! Tanya told me to be careful.

I was so dumb at that time. I had some lumps in my breast, so I had been going to the doctor. My husband never wanted to go with me, but this time he did. The doctor looked at my breasts and said I was fine, that I did not have any cancer and there was nothing to worry about. My husband said, "You mean she does not have cancer?"

The doctor said, "No, she has no cancer."

My husband turned his head and softly said, "Shit!" He always said that word. He loved to say it. It was right after this that he bought the life insurance policy.

When we bought our house, he brought papers for me to sign and I would sign without asking any questions or even looking at the papers. It turned out that the papers were applications for lines of credit. Bills started coming to the house. big bills for like $5,000, but we had nothing. He did not buy me anything to show for these large bills. He had a $50,000 line of credit. When the bills started coming, I told him we had to talk.

"What are all these bills? I don't have anything; I don't see you with anything new. What are these bills?" I asked him.

He left to go to the Montgomery Ward store. He bought me a diamond ring because, I guess, he felt bad. I checked it out and found it cost $399 on sale. Now, I started to wake up.

It was in 1989 when Leon wanted to refinance the house for $50,000. At that time, I had this young black woman who rented a room from us. Her name was Martha.

Martha said, "Maria, don't sign; don't let him borrow this money."

I asked, "What are you talking about?"

She said, "Don't! If you let him borrow this money, he could leave and you will have no more equity."

I went to work and I called him. I said, "What if we go to lunch today, so we can talk?" We met at Denny's. I was doing an import/export business at the time. I told him if we wanted to take $50,000 out of the house, we could open a store for ourselves, instead of working out of the home. We could have our own store.

He said, "That would be nice, but I need the whole $50,000 for something else I need to do." When he said he would not help me with the purchase of a store, I became suspicious.

I said, "Okay, if you want to take money out of this house and if you don't want to help me, I guess we won't take money out of the house."

He said, "Well baby, tell me, how is it your house? Did you pay for it?"

I said, "Well yes, we bought it together. We each put $7,000 down."

He said, "But I am the one who makes the payments." Later that day, he brought a man to the house for me to sign papers for a loan. I was so scared about what he would do if I did not sign the papers. Martha told me to leave the house. I was gone for two hours, but when I returned, the man was still there. I told him I did not want to sign the papers. I told him my husband had refused to loan me the money. Leon turned red. I never signed the papers.

My feelings started to change for my husband. I did not have the love for him I once had. It was like we had separated, but still lived together. We still slept in the same bed, but I would not let him have sex with me. He started to drink and he treated me meanly. I became strong. We did a lot of fighting.

One day, I started adding up everything that had happened: how he left me with the broken door, the life insurance policy on me, how he reacted when the doctor told him I didn't have cancer. I figured it was time for me to get out of there.

It was February, 1990 when I decided to leave and divorce him. It was a nice day—a Sunday. We had kids in the house. I called him outside and said, "How would you feel if we were to get separated? Because the way our marriage has been going, we don't have a marriage. It seems like you are not happy and I know I am not happy." I continued, "If we get separated and you miss me, you call me and we can work it out.

His answer to me was "If we get separated, we might as well get a divorce."

I said to myself, *That is exactly what I want.* But for him, I knew he had a lot of things in his kids' name and in his mom's name, because I was his second wife. I told him we would divide things evenly and that he could either sell me his interest in the house or I would sell him my interest in the house.

He looked at me and said, "Baby, what do you mean your interest in the house? This is my house.

I am the one who worked and paid for everything."

The next morning, I found a lawyer in the yellow pages and made an appointment for the same day. I explained everything to him that had happened. The lawyer prepared a subpoena so that my husband could not take everything. On Sunday I found a lawyer, on Monday I found a house to rent, and on Tuesday I moved.

Chapter 31

TALKS WITH IVAN, 1998

When I came to the U.S., I saw my sibling's father, Ivan Montana again. He always had that smirk on his face, as he remembered what he had done to me. He also knew I remembered what he had done. But I didn't get the chance to confront him about it right away, because we always had someone with us. Then one day he stopped by our house in Roxbury, where I lived with my mom and my sons.

I told him, "I still remember what you did to me!"

He said, "Oh, don't talk about it now. We'll talk about it another time; your mom is coming." We didn't talk about it then, and every time he saw me, he would find some excuse so that we couldn't talk about it. He finally retired and left the States to move back to the islands. In 1998, he returned to visit and also see his doctor. By this time I had moved to California.

I thought about flying back to the East Coast just to talk to him. To tell him especially how I felt about the way he treated me. I was hurt that he promised me so much and then forgot all about me. I didn't have enough money to buy the airline ticket, so I didn't go. When he died, I felt bad. I didn't feel so bad about his dying; I felt bad that I didn't get a chance to talk to him. I never forgot the little white face towel he had sent me. It meant so much to me that I always kept it safe; I never used it. I brought the towel with me when I moved from Cape Verde to Boston in 1969. And when I moved to California in 1980, I know I brought the towel along with me. But in 1999, after Ivan's death, somehow the towel disappeared. I looked everywhere, and I could not find it. The man that I had once thought of as my daddy was gone and the one gift that he had given me that I treasured was gone too.

Chapter 32

Talks with My Sister, 1998

On September 17, 1998, I spoke to my sister, Zita, who lived in Boston. My sister and I began to talk about all the things she saw when we were little. I asked her why they couldn't protect me. My sister explained to me that the adults around me could not protect me because Monster had money and power.

Nothing happened to Zita, but what happened to me affected her. Zita pondered, "Sometimes, I think about what kind of mother could do that to her daughter." I felt that all these things had bothered Zita very much. She told me she remembered the time my mother slapped me to make me go to bed with her boyfriend. Because of what she saw, she had a problem with her sex life. I told her to go to a counselor for help.

Zita said, "Sister, the thing that makes me feel so bad is how they treated me like a queen and they treated you like a slave." I felt good when she admitted this, because this was the way I felt about these things all my life. When she told me this, I was also kind of shocked. She recalled, "I don't know if you remember the time this man had a big, thick stick behind the door. He told me, 'If you don't tell me what Bina be doing when you guys go someplace, I will beat the shit out of you until I make you bleed!'" Sometimes she had to lie. "I couldn't even talk to anyone because they were afraid I would tell someone."

I am five years older than Zita. It took all these years of growing up before we both could talk about this. We were so afraid of Monster we dared not mention anything to anyone. Even in 1998 when we spoke, she had a hard time talking about it because it made her sick. It was so hard to explain my feelings. I knew how much it bothered her, because it bothered me, even though she was not the one who was abused.

I can remember Zita growing up with lots of clothes, lots of gold chains and earrings. I had only two dresses and that was it. I didn't have shoes to put on my feet until I came to the United States at the age of 21. I don't know if there was a reason I should deserve to be treated like that. Maybe there was a reason my mom thought she couldn't make it with her other children and me. Maybe she wished I had died. Zita felt sorry for me that I had such bad luck. She had never seen anyone have as much bad luck as me. Sometimes I think about these things and it makes me so sad. I still have so much in my mind that I have to figure out. It is necessary for me to understand all that happened to me.

On September 27th, 1998, I called my sister Zita's cousin who also lives in Boston. She is older than I am; she is about the age of my sister Maria Julia whom I'm looking for and her name is Maria Julia too. She gave me some of the information I have shared in this book. She gave an account of my birth in 1946 and offered a description of the house I was born in. I remembered what the house looked like because I would often go back to it when I was around nine or ten years old. We spoke for an hour and a half about the rough times our families had back in those days.

I'm glad my sister is old enough now to talk to me about all the things that happened. I was afraid no one would ever believe me if I told my story. My sister knows the truth, but as long as our mom is still alive, she doesn't want to talk about it. When the time comes, I believe Zita will talk about it. I'm not happy about what happened to me, but I am glad I have a sister to talk to. I have someone who saw and knows what happened. I have at least one eyewitness that could verify my story. I know my mom saw much of it, but I can't bring up all the past to her now, especially in her old age.

Zita called my son and talked to him for a while. She told him he should take care of me. She said she didn't know how I was still alive. She thought that with all the abuse I had gone through that I would have committed suicide by now.

Now as a grown woman, I often think that I would like to see Monster again someday. I want to accuse him of all that he did to me and to point out to him how much he hurt me; how wrong he was to abuse an innocent little girl. But then, I think that perhaps I should leave him alone because I might do something foolish. I might try to kill him if I see him again, because of the anger I still have wrapped inside of me. I guess I could write him a letter expressing all the hurt feelings that I carry in my heart and in my mind. Maybe this book will help me in getting out all the hatred that is inside of me. This man abused me, he molested me, and he also raped me of my ability to enjoy what life I could have had.

Chapter 33

TALKS WITH ROY, 1999

January 2, 1999, I'm a 52-year-old lady today. I spoke to my first love, Roy. He came to the U.S. about seven months ago and found a way to call me. We talked a while and Roy reminded me of a lot of things about the past. I call him my first love, but we were never allowed to have any love. I love him, and I will always love him, because he was the only man who didn't take advantage of me. I believe he really loved me. He had the same opportunity to take advantage of me as all of the other men, but he never did.

I remember the time that I met him at the rock ditch, which was near the mountain spring where many people went to get fresh water. Roy held me and I talked to him and told him that my family didn't want me to see him, but I couldn't tell him about the abuse that was happening to me at that time. After we spoke here in the U.S., I told him all about what had happened to me.

He told me he knew that already. He said that was the reason he tried his best to take me away from there, but my mom stood in his way. I was afraid; I was of no help, because I always listened to my mom and the other people more than I listened to him.

Roy used to say, "Bina, come away with me! I promise you I will marry you." But I couldn't, because I was afraid to ask my mother. She was the only person I knew I had. It was a beautiful feeling, a good feeling, and it was sad at the same time as we talked about our past lives. Again, it was so sad, as it reminded me of all the ugliness that I had been through.

I didn't care so much that he didn't marry me; at least he was a man who didn't impose himself on me. No one forced me to be with him. He was one of the few men I knew on the island who didn't want to take advantage of me. I sometimes wish he had taken me, because I'm sure it would have been a much more pleasant experience to be in his strong, but gentle hands. It would have been out of love. Those other men only wanted to rape and molest me for their own pleasure without any consideration of my feelings. I didn't have love in my life as a child and I didn't have love as a teenager.

Chapter 34

TALKS WITH MY MOTHER

I spoke to my mother in Boston, Massachusetts not too long ago. I wanted to ask her one more time about my father's name. She told me my father's name is John. She told me about 20 years ago my father's name was Juan, and she told me again in the past that his name was Edgar. But this day, she said it was John.

I told her, "Mom, I know you are 85 years old, but if you can remember, can you please tell me the name of my father? Which one?"

She said, "It is John." I believe my mom doesn't know for sure what his name is. But I was trying to find out if my father was still alive. If he was still alive, he might be the same age as my mom or maybe a little older. I am not sure. It has been so hard for me to have a father I never met. I have a sister I never met. I am over 50 years old. My life has been so complicated. I hope God is with me to help me till the end of my life to be happy. I deserve that. I deserve all of the happiness I can get.

One thing that I never could talk to my mom about was what Ivan had done to me. I never could face my mom with the truth, though I did get the chance to tell my sister about it. In May of 2002, I told my sister about what happened to me with her dad.

She told me, "I believe you. I believe he was a man capable of doing things like that." I thought we closed the book on that subject. But I came to find out that she told our mom what I had said about Ivan. Mom didn't believe it. She never believed anything I said. She didn't believe me when I was a little kid and she wouldn't believe me today, even though I am a grown woman. I could be here telling her the honest truth and she would just call me a liar.

I am going to make it. I am older and I am stronger now. I am going to continue to be strong. I used to call Mom every Sunday, sometimes two or three times a week. But I found myself resenting her when I started to write about my life, and all the ugliness that went with it. At least for now, I am very upset with her. I don't care anymore. I don't know what to talk about when she calls me. It's kind of strange because it all came back to me. She could have protected me; I was her daughter. I can count just a few men that didn't take advantage of me, who didn't rape me. That was no life for a child. I couldn't do anything. I couldn't scream. No one could hear me anyway.

I'm sure my mom feels guilty now. Every year when I go to visit her in Boston, I feel something when I'm in the room with her. I feel this when I pass by her and the way she looks at me. She won't talk about it. I have thought about talking to her about the past and maybe she might open up, but for some reason I can't bring up the subject. Maybe I'm afraid that because of her age and the guilt she might be feeling, something could happen to her. I am still protecting her. I really don't want anything bad to happen to Mom. I only wish she could have been more protective of me.

I know my mom went through a lot, but the difference is that I know what has happened to me and I don't take it out on my children. I don't abuse or hurt my children. This is why I came to the United States—to protect the children and keep them from getting hurt the best I can.

Chapter 35
LATEST VISIT, 2005

On June 23rd of 2005, I went to Boston to talk to Mom one more time. I had to get things straight between us. I left from Sacramento Airport to Houston, Texas, and had a good flight. My flight from Houston to Boston was scary because before we lifted off, the plane had engine problems and we were told that all had been fixed. We took off and all went well until we had some turbulence and then I got scared. I was thinking I wasn't going to get to see my mother. But everything was all right by the time I arrived in Boston. I was relieved to be on the ground and I started to relax a little.

My nephew, Adam, came to pick me up from the airport and he dropped me off at my brother, Adrian's house. It wasn't until the next evening on the 24th of June, the day of the São João celebration that I got to see my mom. I was up in my room when the senior citizens' van drove up to my brother's house. Two fellows unloaded Mom and carried her up the two flights of stairs because she was too weak to walk. They carried her into the living room and that was when I came down. When Mom saw me, I came closer and said hi to her and she started crying.

She said, "You knew I was coming, but you didn't go out to greet me. Didn't you miss me?" Then I told her that I didn't know exactly what time she was coming.

Then we started to chitchat while everyone was around. My sister-in-law had dinner already prepared so we all went to eat. After dinner, I gave Mom her medication and about half an hour later she asked me to take her to the bathroom. I wheeled her to the bathroom in her wheelchair and helped her because she no longer had the strength to help herself. So, at this time, while I was trying to help her I realized that this situation that she was in was the best time to talk to her. I had a hard time picking her up. Not that Mom is very heavy, but because of my weak arm; I just couldn't pick her up very easily.

Mom said, "What's the matter? I'm not that heavy, am I?"

I said, "No, Mom." And we both started to laugh. Then I called my brother to help me.

He said, "Now she needs two people to help her."

Finally, about an hour later, everyone left to go to the São João celebration, but I chose to stay home with Mom.

It was kind of hard to find the words to talk to her, but after a while I sat close to her and gently I asked her, "Mom, do you remember Monster?"

She replied, "Yes, I cannot forget him." Then she asked, "Why do you ask? He died a long time ago."

I said, "I wanted to know because I still remember all those terrible things that he did to me."

She asked, "What things?"

I told her, "Mom, you know what things, because you were there."

She said, "You're a liar!"

Then I said, "Mom, if you remember him, you should remember that you helped him." She said, "Even if it's true, what do you want me to do? You want me to put him in jail?" I said, "Now, it's too late!"

She said, "Bina, it was a time of hunger. There was no sugar, no beans, no rice, no potatoes—nothing to eat. He provided us with all those things."

Then I asked, "But Mom, why did it have to be me? You were still young. You could go to work and bring those things home."

She said, "Shut up! Why don't you remember Joãozinho? Why didn't you call the police on him?"

I explained, " I was only nine or ten years old. That was your job." She continued to deny everything I said. But I told her, "Mom, you knew Joãozinho was going there just to get me. But you didn't do anything about it."

She said, "Yes, I know, but what did you want me

to do?" Again, she was denying her responsibility in everything, but at the same time, she knew all these things that happened were true.

I realized that she remembered everything, because during our conversation she mentioned Monster, Joãozinho, and other names that I didn't even remember. I was so young; I didn't remember all of the men.

Then she said, "For you to talk to me like this, to ask me these kinds of questions, why don't you just kick my ass?"

I looked at her and laughed and said, "You just cannot change."

She said, "This is the present you brought me from California. You have a big mouth and you talk too much. You don't see why your sister Zita don't talk to you?"

I said, "No! I don't see why. Why, because I tell the truth? This is why? Because the truth hurts! You hurt right now, because you know I'm telling the truth."

Then finally, she said, "Why don't you talk about your uncle?"

I said, "Yes, Mom, I'm glad you mentioned that. Because my uncle was set up, and you know that."

She looked at me and said, "What?"

I said, "You know that you and Monster, and Daisy, were together in setting up Uncle José."

Then it seemed as if Mom was surprised to hear this. It looked like she really thought it was true about

166

Uncle José touching me inappropriately and it wasn't.

After my Uncle's funeral, I talked to my cousin Maria Alves, and she told me, "When your mom went to the house, she was crying very hard, painfully crying as they laid her down in her bed. She kept saying, 'Forgive me, José; forgive me, José.' She said it three or four times."

I asked, "Why couldn't my mom have said that while your dad was alive?"

My cousin answered, "Well, at least she said it. And I know he will forgive her, where he is now."

Chapter 36

FOSTERING TEENAGE GIRLS

I'm going to skip some things from this story of my life because I want to add something positive. I cannot keep going on with these negative things. Now is the time to mention some of the positive things that have happened to me.

I started to do foster parenting in 1990. I have taken care of a lot of children, a lot of babies. I felt so great when I had those babies in the house. I didn't enjoy seeing them in their predicament, but I felt good about being able to help them. I was happy that I was the one they chose to come to for help taking care of these displaced kids.

One day I sat down with the teenagers I had at that time in my care. One of the teens went for a walk and about forty-five minutes later, she came back home. Her name was Shaquilla. She sat down on the floor and she started crying her heart out.

I looked at her and asked her, "Why do you cry?"

She said, "Why do you ask? You don't care. You don't care why I cry, so why do you ask?"

I said, "Hey, you want to try me? Do you think I don't care? If I didn't care I wouldn't be asking. Get off the floor, come sit on the couch with me, and talk to me about it."

She said, "I just let him do it."

I said, "What were you doing?"

Shaquilla said, "I just let him do it."

I said, "Why did you let him do it? Did he force you?"

She responded, "No!"

I asked, "Then why did you let him do it?"

She said, "Because he said he loved me. You don't understand. I'm looking for love."

Oh, my God! My thoughts went straight to myself. This was the reason I needed to find. It was my foster children who helped me realize it. I was trying to help them, and in turn they helped me. It was these children who helped me realize that I was not the only child who had gone through what I had gone through. My life may have been more difficult and filled with a lot more stuff happening all at the same time, but they had many of the same kinds of problems that I had.

I held Shaquilla and we hugged each other and then sat back down on the couch to talk. I shared some of my story with her which made both of us cry.

Shaquilla was 18 years old; this was her last year in the foster care system. She left after that and I have not seen her since, but she has written me three times.

There was another foster child; a girl who called me today and we spoke about some of her problems. She told me that she felt that her sexual violence problems had a lot to do with her mother and having a lot of boyfriends. She was another one who reminded me of my past. These teenagers helped me become determined in wanting to help others by telling my story. I want to do my best to bring my story to the reading public so that other women can learn to stand up for themselves and not to take it as I did. We need to educate women that they are allowed to talk. They have the right to seek help. They have the right to seek shelter from those who mean to harm them. Women need to help each other and find ways to stand strong so that they are not defeated one by one in isolation.

Chapter 37

THE VISITOR

All of my life I have had a connection to the other side. I believe it is God and my guardian angel taking care of me. I sometimes can see things other people don't see, I have dreams about things that will happen and I get feelings that warn me to be careful. Sometimes I don't understand what's going on and other times it makes a lot of sense.

It was one summer evening in about 1984 when I was getting ready to take a friend and her grandson home. We were standing in my driveway and for some reason I looked toward my bedroom window. I saw a shadow in the window that looked just like Michael Jackson. I couldn't believe it. Why was there a shadow of Michael Jackson coming from my bedroom window?

I have always loved Michael Jackson and his music and his song *Billie Jean* was my favorite. I felt that we had a connection because we both loved kids. When we got in the car, I wanted to ask my friend if she saw something too, but I didn't want to sound crazy and say it was Michael. So I asked, "Did you see something in my bedroom window?"

She said, "Yes!"

I said, "What did it look like?"

She said, "It looked like Michael Jackson wearing clothes from the video for *Billie Jean*—same hair, same everything!"

Now I knew I wasn't going crazy. My friend's grandson was in the back seat and he said he saw the same thing. It was so strange. I couldn't figure out why he would show up in my window. I didn't tell very many people because they wouldn't believe me anyway, but my friend saw him too.

A few years later when he was accused of molestation, I didn't believe it. I couldn't believe it. When he died in 2009, I felt so bad. I was sad for a long time and had pains in my chest when I would think about him.

Right after he passed away and before they buried him, I saw him again. It was about 2:30 in the morning and I was asleep in my bed. I heard someone come into my room and stand next to the bed. I moved a little bit and heard a noise. I have a statue of the Virgin Mary in my room and I opened my eyes and looked at the statue. The Virgin Mary's face had changed a little bit! I closed my eyes and heard the noise again, so I sat up on the edge of my bed and looked at the statue.

This time the Virgin Mary's face looked just like Michael Jackson.

I asked, "Is that you, Michael?" and then the statue changed back. Now, why would Michael Jackson come to visit me? I feel like he knew I worked with kids as a foster parent and how much I liked him. I think we had a lot in common as children and had a connection. I always regretted that I never met him.

Chapter 38

FOSTER MOM

I have been a foster parent now for quite a few years. I always teach my foster kids that when someone tries to touch you in the wrong way, you must talk about it. Go to the teacher, call the police, call anybody, but don't let anybody get away with hurting you, not even once. It has taken me so many years to be able to talk about the things that happened to me. I was so embarrassed. I felt bad; I didn't want anybody to know about it. I wanted to hide.

I take care of children from the ages of one to nineteen. I have had a lot of children who have been through similar situations. I don't want any children to hurt anymore. I want to teach kids how to take care of themselves, to protect themselves, and to speak up for themselves.

I pray to God every day to thank him that I have survived. I am a stronger person now, a strong surviving woman. Then again, I have to be if I want to be a successful foster parent. I was only three and half but I can remember it very clearly. I don't want little children or teenagers to go through the abuse or molestation I went through.

I have always taught my foster children don't let that person get away with abusing them and then be free to abuse some other child. The first time it happens, talk about it so it doesn't happen a second time. I know because it has taken me so many years to learn how to talk about what happened to me. Even as I got older, into my twenties, I had nobody to talk to, no one to listen to me. But maybe I didn't look hard enough to find the help I needed.

Chapter 39

HELPING OTHER WOMEN

I give God thanks every day because I'm still alive. I give Him thanks because I am blessed. I would really love to help other women and children. Be it boys or girls, teenagers or adults, the age doesn't matter because no one deserves to be in any kind of abusive situation, particularly not in a sexual one.

I've prayed to God to help me get my story out of the shadows of my mind and bring it out into the open so that others will feel free and encouraged to speak up about their lives and situations. I hope to enable other victims of abuse to stand up for themselves and become strong enough to help others to end abusive cycles.

Keeping it all hidden inside of us will cause us not to help ourselves and not help anyone else. I would like to get my story on a national TV program that would reach millions of people. With faith in God and my guardian angel, in the name of Jesus Christ, I will get my story out to the people someday. This isn't for me; it is a chance to help the many, many others who are out there without a voice. I know that I am not the only one with this kind of a story, not the only one who has been sexually abused and was too afraid to speak about it. I am now telling the truth about what happened to me only after more than fifty years of being ashamed and embarrassed about it.

I'm no longer ashamed because I do believe I need to get help. I didn't have any rights as a child to preserve my own body from abuse. All the abuse caused me to grow up with an inferiority complex, a lack of trusting men, and a fear of sexual relationships. I need help now for my future, so that I may one day be a whole person content to be in my own skin and content to be with someone I can love and trust as a sexual partner. It is no wonder that my sexual relationships have been the most troubling.

And I thank God for it

And I thank God for all that happened to me. I'm still able to help other people. I try to be as helpful as I can. I don't have much myself, but I take money out of my pocket and give to the poor. I feel that I can give what I have to those less fortunate than myself. I have taken food out of my freezer and have given it to the poor. I try to be helpful by cooking extra food for the holidays to give to others who are needy. I usually pick families that have more children in the house to bring food to them. It makes me feel good. I thank God for it.

Thank God that I am a strong woman and I can hold my head high with a smile on my face and look forward to another day, as well as have hope for the future. I thank God for the blessings that he has given me from my children and the children I take care of to the roof over our heads. I thank him for giving me strength and keeping me going and living day by day.

CPSIA information can be obtained
at www.ICGtesting.com
Printed in the USA
BVHW060210180220
572581BV00011B/1191